Exploring Verbal Cues to Deception:
Testing Quantitative Linguistic Methods on English and Spanish

I0577033

Ángela Almela Sánchez-Lafuente

# Exploring Verbal Cues to Deception: Testing Quantitative Linguistic Methods on English and Spanish

PETER LANG

**Bibliographic Information published by the
Deutsche Nationalbibliothek**
The Deutsche Nationalbibliothek lists this publication in the Deutsche
Nationalbibliografie; detailed bibliographic data is available online at
http://dnb.d-nb.de.

**Library of Congress Cataloging-in-Publication Data**
A CIP catalog record for this book has been applied for at the
Library of Congress.

ISBN 978-3-0343-4188-2 (Print)
E-ISBN 978-3-0343-4711-2 (E-PDF)
E-ISBN 978-3-0343-4712-9 (EPUB)
DOI 10.3726/b20697

© Peter Lang Group AG, International Academic Publishers,
Bern 2023
www.peterlang.com.

This publication has been peer reviewed.

www.peterlang.com

# EXPLORING VERBAL CUES TO DECEPTION:

# TESTING QUANTITATIVE LINGUISTIC METHODS

# ON ENGLISH AND SPANISH

Ángela Almela

## DEDICATION

This book is dedicated to my late father. He lives on most vividly in the realm of memory, and he will always be an endless source of love and wisdom to me.

# CONTENTS

# ACKNOWLEDGMENTS

This book marks the culmination of several years of hard work. This would not have been possible without the insights and support I received from wonderful people who must be acknowledged here. First and foremost, I am especially grateful to Pascual Cantos, PhD and Rafael Valencia-García, PhD, who generously provided insights and guidance during the preparation of an earlier version of this work for submission as a doctoral thesis. I would not be where I am today without their mentoring.

I am also happy to acknowledge the expert help of Carole E. Chaski, PhD, who has been strongly supportive to me. Likewise, it is with a genuine sense of gratitude that I report the financial support provided by the Institute for Linguistic Evidence. My special thanks go to this scientific research organization for providing vital research funds and enthusiastic support during these years of hard work, and for surmounting the difficulties to promote a paradigm shift in the application of linguistics as a forensic science.

Furthermore, I am very much indebted to Dr. Carlo Strapparava, Dr. Rada Mihalcea, and Sgt. Larry Barskdale, MA, as they shared their linguistic corpora with me, making part of this project possible.

Special thanks go to the management teams of the College of Arts and Humanities of Universidad de Murcia (Facultad de Letras, *Delta Force*) and of the Department of English Studies (Filología Inglesa, *Filing Power*) for their trust in me, as well as their close interest in my research throughout the project.

I have also had the pleasure of working with the capable editing team at Peter Lang, and my thanks in particular go to Ulrike Döring and her team for their empathy and practical assistance.

I have a warm feeling of gratitude towards Sam, who has been a virtual witness to countless hours of work and a faithful companion during this lengthy process (you know, *yo he venido aquí a hablar de mi libro*). I owe my thanks to him and to all my friends, as they are one of my most valuable assets.

Moreover, I am particularly indebted to my family for being always there with support and love. I am more than grateful for Miguel's backing, and for being a committed husband, father and friend all these years.

Finally, a special mention goes to Mario and Eduardo, who inspire me every day to juggle the responsibilities of motherhood, professorship, and college administration while trying to remain grounded.

# CHAPTER 1. Introduction

## 1.1 Deception and language

The distinction between truth and deception has captured considerable attention from different domains, and the popularity enjoyed by deception detection has transcended formal research, reaching popular culture and giving rise to several forms of entertainment such as "cheap" or "paperback" literature; it has even reached the television industry, becoming the central theme of different TV series[1] or of the well-known show *Lie Detector,* where tools like the polygraph are used to check the veracity of the statements made by both the general public and important figures. However, this increasing appeal of deception detection has also fed widely held myths into the popular consciousness. For instance, most people think that a liar can often be spotted just by observing their behavior. Most relevantly, in the majority of cases, it is felt that, as Vrij (2010: 1) ironically puts it, "[f]ortunately, we are well protected against them, because professional lie catchers are good at spotting such liars." Nonetheless, this is just practitioners' and researchers' desideratum.

The investigation of linguistic cues to deception in written language is of utmost importance, not only in the forensic context with statements written by

---

[1] An example is the TV series *Lie to Me*, created by Samuel Baum (Imagine Entertainment, 20th Century Fox Television).

1

witnesses and people implicated in crimes, but also because of the increase seen by computer-mediated communication, where written texts constitute a fundamental element.

Nevertheless, the substantial body of literature on deception detection which is currently available should not mean that all is said in this field. Certain aspects of this area have not received enough attention. For instance, it is worth noting the lack of research into this issue from a discursive perspective, exploring the potential linguistic variations according to the topic dealt with. Last but not least, as mentioned above, most machine learning approaches to the issue at hand have not given a comprehensive description of the linguistic cues to deception at a contrastive linguistics level, but have rather dealt with broader dimensions in a single language.

Extensive research has been conducted into the linguistic nature of deception, addressing the question of whether deceptive statements are deviant enough to betray insincere speakers. Experimental findings on the distinctive features seem to conflict, hence the skepticism towards this line of research voiced by certain scholars such as Vartapetiance and Gillam (2012). The present monograph presents an approach in which deception in written language is not explored as a whole but taking into consideration the particular modality of the corpus and the discursive differences among topics.

## 1.2 Aims of the book

This monograph makes a substantial contribution to the study of computational linguistic tools as an aid to deception detection and deepens the readers' understanding of the linguistic mechanisms underlying deceit. Unlike most Machine Learning (ML) approaches to the issue at hand, it offers a comprehensive description of the linguistic cues to deception and promotes a contextualized study of deception, rather than dealing with broader dimensions of analysis. By tackling this issue, I hope to deepen the reader's understanding of the linguistic mechanisms underlying deceit. It is hoped that forensic linguists, jurists, lawyers, computational linguists, and psychologists may benefit from this study.

## 1.3 Structure of the book

This monograph is structured as follows. Chapter 2 provides the theoretical background necessary to understand and evaluate the findings of the empirical studies presented in Chapters 3, 4 and 5. Specifically, Chapter 3 presents the research questions and the methods which have been followed in order to carry out the study. The aim of the study is to explore the linguistic cues to deception in written language, performing a contrastive analysis between (1) English and Spanish; (2) low-stakes and high-stakes in English. Study 1 (cross-linguistic experiment) can be found in Chapter 4, including discussion of the results, and Study 2 is presented in Chapter 5. Finally, having considered the results obtained, some final remarks are provided in Chapter 6. Furthermore, the major limitations of both studies are exposed and some plausible lines for further research are advanced.

# CHAPTER 2. Deception, its nature and its detection

## 2.1 Shaping deception

In the context of human communication, deception plays an active role. Indeed, DePaulo et al. (1996) report that people tell an average of one to two lies a day, the context of mediated communication not being an exception (Hancock, Thom-Santelli and Ritchie, 2004). The philosophical discussion of lying to others and interpersonal deceiving mainly involves definitional questions. As Mahon (2015) puts it in the *Stanford Encyclopedia of Philosophy*, this group includes the questions of how lying and deceiving are to be defined; other questions relevant to the philosophical discussion of lying to others and other-deception are moral, including whether lying and deceiving are morally wrong. Due to the linguistic nature of this research monograph, only questions of the first kind are considered here.

Although there is no universally accepted definition of lying (Kagan, 1998), Mahon (2015: 3) advances that the most common one is as follows: "to make a believed-false statement to another person with the intention that that other person believe that statement to be true" (see Fig. 2.1). Accordingly, for lying there would be four necessary conditions: a statement given by a person; the untruthfulness condition of the statement; the requirement that the untruthful statement be made to another person or addressee; and the intention to deceive the addressee. Castelfranchi and Poggi (2002) insist on the last

5

condition, stating that the deceiver's intention must be part of the definition. They clearly distinguish this purposeful act from misinformation which is perpetuated by mistake or not trying to mislead the recipient, which is not to be deemed as deception. On the contrary, truthful messages intentionally conveyed in the belief that they are untruthful are usually considered to be a form of deception (DePaulo et al., 2003).

Fig. 2.1. Graphical depiction of deception (retrieved and adapted from https://www.vecteezy.com/free-vector/deception).

This is the definition of deception used in this monograph, since it necessarily involves the intention to communicate with another person by means of a statement, which is more than adequate for automated linguistic detection methods. Other forms of deception like omissions are more difficult to detect through these means. However, this does not imply that deception in the broadest sense of the term is to be identified with outright falsification. The former may be considered to be the hypernym and the latter just one of its potential hyponyms. This means in practice that it is possible to mislead others by means of further strategies like ambiguity or exaggeration (Burgoon, Buller and Woodall, 1996). In this respect, Jensen (2007: 29) provides a comprehensive list of the methods used to deceive; Table 2.1 shows an adaptation.

| Methods of deception |
| --- |
| Fabrications |
| Evasions |
| Equivocation |
| Concealments |
| Exaggerations |
| Omissions |
| Camouflage |
| Misdirection |
| Strategic ambiguity |
| Bluffs |
| Hoaxes |
| Tall tales |
| Charades |
| White lies |
| Sophistry |
| Half-truths |

Table 2.1 List of methods of deception (adapted from Jensen, 2007).

## 2.2 The study of deception

The empirical study of deception in language dates at least from Undeutsch (1967), who firmly believed in the existence of certain criteria for the configuration of the truthfulness of statements. Some years later, he would formulate what is nowadays known as the *Undeutsch hypothesis*: "a statement derived from a memory of an actual experience differs in content and quality from a statement based on invention or fantasy" (Undeutsch, 1989: 102). Since then, this line of research has shown that deceivers somewhat differ in verbal, visual and physiological behavior from truth-tellers. The identification of the key cues to deception has been commonplace in forensic linguistics, especially in the English-speaking world. Thus, several studies have been devoted to the assessment of human ability to detect lies. According to Vrij et al. (2000), most pieces of research report accuracy rates ranging from 45% to 60%, with a mean accuracy rate of 56.6%, which shows that, in practice, it rarely performs above chance. As for the performance of college students in comparison to police officers, studies like Kassin et al. (2005) showed that the former were generally more accurate than the latter.

More recently, researchers have become increasingly interested in the development and evaluation of automated tools for identifying lies, giving rise to automated and computer-aided deception detection. This discipline may benefit from several areas of natural language processing, such as automated text classification, opinion mining and sentiment analysis, as well as linguistic areas like discourse analysis, pragmatics and phonetics. The potential

8

applications of automated and computer-aided deception detection cover the areas of law enforcement, advertising, computer-mediated communication, national security, and human resources, to name but a few.

Non-verbal language makes up about two-thirds of all human communication. Probably due to its importance, research on deception detection has mostly focused on physiological cues, which has led to the creation and use of several tools such as the polygraph. More recently, researchers have begun to explore the identification of verbal cues which are useful for separating truth from lies, mainly in oral language.

### 2.2.1 Theories of deception

Several theories of deception have provided the guiding foundation for methods of deception detection. In this section, the four major theories will be reviewed: leakage theory, Zuckerman's four-factor model of deception, interpersonal deception theory, and the self-presentational view.

Ekman and Friesen (1969) first noted that deception could be made evident through unaware physical behavior. According to the authors, lying can manifest itself through two different types of behavioral cues. First, deception may become obvious through physical leakage cues. This type of cue arises when deceivers attempt to conceal their spontaneous reactions and true emotions. This notion led to the study of micromomentary facial expressions as a method for lie detection (Jensen, 2007). Second, deception cues refer to the absence of natural movements commonly displayed by speakers during truthful interaction. In an attempt to control their non-verbal behavior, deceivers usually show unnatural body stiffness which itself may be betraying. In this respect, DePaulo and Kirkendol (1989) explain that motivated deceivers trying to control their demeanor behave differently from those who do not try to cover it up. Thus, the least successful ones are motivated deceivers (usually in high-stakes situations) involved in oral interactions. This approach to deception is commonly known as leakage theory.

Some years later, Ekman (1985) first provided evidence to support Zuckerman's four-factor model of deception (1981). This model relies upon four different factors: arousal, emotion, cognitive effort, and attempted control of behavior. These psychological areas are readily susceptible to variations during deceptive communication. According to this theory, higher levels of arousal and negative emotions are usually observed, increased cognitive load is shown, as well as a lack of spontaneity, resulting from the deliberate attempt to control non-verbal behavior. However, this model has its detractors, especially concerning the first factor. As explained above, Mann, Vrij and Bull (2002) suggest that deceivers do not necessarily feel nervous when involved in high-stakes situations, since some of them happen to be highly experienced liars. Furthermore, an anxious interviewee is not always a deceiving one, and vice versa.

Buller and Burgoon (1996) discuss that the different ways of lying do not occur per se, but that the context where the lie is uttered plays a major role, formulating their interpersonal deception theory (IDT) within the context of interpersonal communication. They argue that lying is adaptable and that different issues should be considered, such as the deceiver's motivation to lie; the consequences for liars in the event of being caught; the degree of formality of the situation; and the existing relationship between deceiver and deceived, to name but a few. Even personality plays a role in producing language, like in the dichotomy introversion-extraversion, hence its influence on the manner of deceiving (Campbell and Pennebaker, 2003; Pennebaker and King, 1999). Thus, this model emphasizes the deceiver's multiple roles of monitoring, interpreting and adapting untruthful messages taking into account the immediate feedback received.

It is worth noting that IDT presents deception as a strategic interaction among participants, resulting in a more holistic approach to deception than the previous ones. At a global level, the model considers that participants in the interaction bring with them cognitive and affective processes such as their expectations or detection apprehension, as well as their behavioral patterns – e.g. their skills. After an initial behavioral display, the deceiver tries certain strategies which may be modified depending on the feedback received from the recipient, hence the importance of their management of information, images and behavior. This bidirectional feedback is obtained through the leakage of nonstrategic behaviors by both parties. Interestingly enough, the role of the recipient in this model is properly explored too, not only regarding the feedback provided, but also the elements leading to deception detection accuracy on their part. Accordingly, Buller and Burgoon (1996) assure that the recipient gets involved in interaction with a certain level of suspicion –although they allow for the possibility of level zero. Within their cognitions, credibility judgements may result in a modification of this level of suspicion. Regarding the recipient's behavioral patterns, they mainly include suspicion display and uncertainty management. In post-interaction, both parties will evaluate their success at their respective roles.

Finally, DePaulo et al. (2003) propound the self-presentational view of deception, on the grounds that deceivers and truth-tellers hold different beliefs, referred to by the authors as deception discrepancy. They explain the two main implications of this theory as follows: "First, deceptive self-presentations are often not as convincingly embraced as truthful ones. Second, social actors typically experience a greater sense of deliberateness when their performances are deceptive than when they are honest" (DePaulo et al., 2003: 77). This discrepancy notwithstanding, deceivers must project a convincing impression, which generates five categories of cues: they are expected to appear less communicative than truth-tellers; they are predicted to show a more negative attitude; they will probably display a higher level of anxiety; their accounts are expected to be less convincing than truthful ones, as well as to contain a limited amount of sensory details as compared to truthful accounts. Furthermore, the authors highlight the role of motivation to succeed.

## 2.2.2 Professional methods of deception detection

Nowadays, there are a considerable number of methods of deception detection, but only a few are regularly used by professional lie-catchers. Some others have been proposed by professionals and scholars, but their application to real world situations is virtually null. These methods are usually classified into two broad categories: physiological and behavioral methods (see Table 2.2). The former category includes polygraph, brain activity analysis, thermal analysis, and voice stress analysis. Statement validity assessment, linguistic analysis and behavioral analysis are comprised within the latter group. A basic description of these methods is provided in the following sections.

| Physiological methods | Behavioral methods | |
|---|---|---|
| Polygraph | Nonverbal assessment tools | |
| Brain activity analysis | Verbal assessment tools | Statement Validity Assessment |
| Thermal analysis | | Reality Monitoring |
| Voice stress analysis | | Linguistic analysis |

Table 2.2 Methods of deception detection

The development of physiological methods relies on the assumption that arousal, emotions and cognitive changes associated with deception, relevant to Zuckerman's four-factor model of deception, generate systematic physiological changes in aspects such as blood flow, hemo-oxygenation and neuronal activity (Vrij et al., 2000). This has resulted in a wide array of methods, the origins of

13

which lie in the most rudimentary techniques, such as the holding of an ostrich's egg during a suspect's confession –its breaking would be considered to be a reflection of the suspect's arousal, allegedly provoked by deception.

Nowadays, sophisticated technologies are available for the purpose of spotting liars. Probably the most popular physiological method is the polygraph, also known as a lie detector. This device is able to assess parameters such as palmar sweat or heart rate by virtue of sensors attached to the body, an increase of which is an alleged physical response to the human arousal generated by feelings of guilt (Vrij et al., 2000). Both the Control Question Test (CQT) and the Guilty Knowledge Test (GKT) –also known as the Concealed information test– are interviewing methods which involve the use of a polygraph. In their study on this tool and its limits, Faigman, Fienberg and Stern (2003) explain that in the former method the functioning of the polygraph is adjusted by means of a set of control questions in which the subject is deliberately asked to lie. Thus, the level of arousal from these questions is taken as a baseline to draw a comparison with real questions. As far as the GKT is concerned, as suggested by its name, "it determines whether an interviewee has knowledge about a crime that would only be known to the perpetrator" (Jensen, 2007: 37). According to Faigman et al. (2003), this interviewing method is deemed more objective and scientific by experts in the field.

However, the polygraph as an investigative tool suffers from two major serious drawbacks. On one hand, one of the major problems with this method seems to be the large proportion of false positives obtained, being better at detecting fear than deception. On the other hand, several studies have showed that even skilled examiners cannot often determine when subjects use countermeasures to defeat the polygraph. For instance, Honts et al. (1985; 1994) reported that around 50% of guilty subjects in laboratory studies could defeat a polygraph test by engaging in countermeasures such as curling toes inside one's shoes, biting one's tongue, or doing mental arithmetic during control questions in order to provide a fake baseline. Thus, there is extensive criticism leveled at the polygraph for being unreliable and non-scientific, despite its widespread use in certain countries.

As shown in Table 2.2, there are other physiological methods for lie detection, such as those relying on the analysis of brain activity. For instance, Farwell and Donchin (1991) report that the results from criminal applications involving electroencephalograms (EEGs) to measure event-related brain potentials (ERPs) are almost as accurate as the polygraph. Similarly, functional magnetic resonance imaging (fMRI) is also based on the analysis of brain activity, although nowadays its reliability is being questioned, which has led to the investigation of some alternatives to this technique, such as near-infrared spectroscopy (NIRS). In Jensen's words (2007: 38), "NIRS does not require people to remain stationary and uses optical technology to measure neuronal, metabolic, and hemodynamic changes that may indicate arousal associated with deception."

On the other hand, Pavlidis and Levine (2002) designed and tested a promising thermal image analysis method for polygraph testing. As the authors

15

have it, this method "can serve as an additional channel for increasing the reliability and accuracy of traditional polygraph examination" (2002: 1). Specifically, it involves the extraction of subtle facial temperature fluctuation patterns through nonlinear heat transfer modelling, based on the assumption that an increase in the level of arousal caused by deception manifests itself through an instantaneous periorbital warming pattern.

Last but not least, voice stress analysis (VSA) assumes that the psychological stress experienced by deceivers forces certain changes in blood circulation, physiologically reflected by an elevated voice pitch (Vrij, 2010). Significantly enough, in most studies on this technique, researchers have been unable to prove its efficacy (Gamer et al., 2006), mainly due to the large proportion of false positives obtained.

As regards behavioral methods, physiological veracity assessment tools deal with the body functions of human beings. When it comes to behavioral methods, the object of study is the range of actions and mannerisms made in deceptive interactions. In this category, the term behavior comprises two subcategories: the first one deals with the analysis of non-verbal language, whereas the second subcategory is concerned with the assessment of verbal communication. As shown in Table 2.2, the latter group comprises Statement Validity Assessment, Reality Monitoring and linguistic analysis.

The exploration of non-verbal cues has been widely used as a method of deception detection, either in isolation (e.g. Bond and Robinson, 1988; Burgoon et al., 1996; Ekman and Friesen, 1969; Meservy, 2007) or in combination with the role of verbal cues (e.g. Brownsell and Bull, 2011; Ebesu and Miller, 1994; Kraut, 1978; Vrij et al., 2000). Despite the extensive research conducted on non-verbal cues to deception, the lack of consistency in the findings hinders their application to professional practice.

Regarding verbal assessment tools, Statement Validity Assessment (SVA) is the most widely used of these tools, since, as Vrij puts it, it is "accepted as evidence in some North American courts and in criminal courts in several Western European countries, including Austria, Germany, Sweden, Switzerland and the Netherlands" (2010: 201). The SVA method is based on the Undeutsch hypothesis, which, as advanced in section 2.2, concerns the divergence in content and quality of outright fabrications from truthful statements. Specifically, it was designed to determine the credibility of children's statements in sexual offence trials (Trankell, 1972).

Within SVA, Criteria-Based Content Analysis (CBCA) is the core phase. It takes place after a case-file analysis and a semi-structured interview. In this phase, the interviewer assesses the quality of the statements in a systematic fashion by means of transcripts, scoring responses according to an inventory of nineteen predefined criteria such as quantity of details, descriptions of interactions, related external associations, spontaneous corrections, and details characteristic of the offence (for a comprehensive list see Steller and Köhnken, 1989). As opposed to physiological methods of deception detection, interviewees' non-verbal behavior is not evaluated. This allows the interviewer to give undivided attention to linguistic content, which is deemed convenient by most SVA experts (Vrij, 2010). Interestingly enough, all CBCA criteria indicate truth, thus, strictly speaking, it cannot be considered a deception detection method. In Ruby and Brigham's words, "the presence of one of these specific content characteristics indicates a truthful statement while the absence of them indicates nothing" (1994: 18).

A further verbal veracity assessment tool which uses a scoring mechanism to judge statements is Reality Monitoring (RM). Originally, it was mainly concerned with the different cognitive processes involved in the narration of perceived and imagined events (Sporer, 1997). Unlike SVA, professional practitioners do not use RM for lie detection. However, Vrij insists that this tool has become increasingly popular within the field, and that "it has attracted the attention of scientists worldwide, and to date researchers from Canada, Finland, France, Germany, Spain, Sweden, and the United Kingdom have published RM deception research" (2010: 261). Specifically, RM judges expect verbal recalls of actual events to include a greater deal of sensory, contextual, and affective information.

A feature shared by RM and CBCA is that both methods involve working with transcripts, hence the preclusion of non-verbal language in the analysis. Furthermore, despite the absence of a standardized set of RM criteria, some of them overlap with some CBCA criteria. Broadly speaking, RM experts expect certain criteria to occur more often in truthful statements, namely clarity, perceptual information, spatial information, temporal information, affect, reconstructability of the story, and realism. On the contrary, cognitive

18

operations used to be considered characteristic of untruthful statements within this theory, although, as will be seen in subsequent chapters of this work, several studies have obtained the opposite results (e.g. Granhag, Strömwall and Olsson, 2001; Memon et al., 2010).

Last but not least, linguistic analysis is also based on the premise that fabricated messages qualitatively differ from truthful ones. Nonetheless, a crucial difference from the previous methods is worth highlighting: linguistic analyses operate independently of message meaning. Jensen (2007) establishes two broad categories in linguistic analysis: message feature mining and speech act profiling. Firstly, researchers dealing with message feature mining attempt to determine the truth value of the statements by virtue of objective features extracted from the text. Often, this kind of research is not enshrined in any preconceived deception theory, and makes use of certain software applications specifically developed for its purposes or subsequently adapted. By and large, empirical deception studies which apply an automated method for detecting linguistic cues in text independent of context fall within this group, including the experiments performed in the present work. On the other hand, speech act profiling is a method of conversation classification devised by Twitchell et al. (2004). Thus, the main purpose of this method is to make clear the speaker's intention, so as to explore the role of pragmatics in the configuration of linguistic deception.

## 2.3 Research on verbal cues to deception: state of the art

In the last decade, the field of Natural Language Processing (henceforth, NLP) has devoted considerable attention to the automatization of the process of deception detection, developing and employing a wide array of automated and computer-assisted methods for this purpose (e.g., Ott et al., 2011; Quijano-Sánchez et al., 2018). Vogler and Pearl (2019) provide a thorough review of this activity. Similarly, another emerging research area focuses on computer-assisted deception detection using linguistics (e.g., Chaski et al., 2015; Picornell, 2013), with promising results. Thus, some computational approaches supervised by experts in the field are considered as an efficient way to supplement and support criminal investigators, being of special interest to linguists, jurists, criminologists, and professionals in the field of communications.

Accordingly, an overall review of the state of the art regarding linguistic cues to deception is provided in this section, as well as an overview on several approaches to the study of deception and on previous research into its linguistic detection, describing the main controversies in the area (2.3.1 and 2.3.2). In line with the literature review supplied in Almela (2021a), the present author draws a distinction between software packages specifically developed for linguistic deception detection and other verbal assessment tools which are widely used for this and many other purposes (2.3.3). Furthermore, this section advances some prime considerations that, from the present author's viewpoint, must be taken into account when conducting research in this area. For a whole account of theories and controversies in the area of deception detection in general, the reader may resort to Meibauer (2018), which reports past and current research on all aspects of lying and deception, as it is a comprehensive exploration of the state of the art from the combined perspectives of linguistics, philosophy, and psychology.

### 2.3.1 Essentials of forensic computational linguistics

The grounds of this section are to be set on the concept of linguistics as a science. First of all, it is important to bear in mind that in forensic computational linguistics, methods must be tested by experiments, and that there is a great advantage brought by the fact that nowadays some linguistic methods can be automated in software (Chaski, 2020). Thus, the present approach is intimately related to corpus linguistics (henceforth, CL), which can be applied to different aspects of language (e.g., any level of language analysis and any focus of language use). Leaving theoretical controversies aside, researchers seem to agree that CL provides an objective view of language that overcomes a single scholar's introspection, by the systematic examination of a collection of texts (corpus) used to find the answer to a research question related to patterns of language in use.

CL approaches are based on two main principles: empiricism and technology. As for the former, CL is essentially empirical. This means that it explores language in context, or the performance of language, recalling the

Chomskyan distinction between performance –what people do linguistically– and competence –what people know implicitly of language (Chomsky, 1957). In this line of thought, Leech (1992) remarked that CL examines a question of performance, of language in use. The analysis is therefore based on observation and experience, from which theoretical principles can be formulated. In this sense, the approach is "bottom-up." CL can also be seen as a tool in "top-down" approaches, since CL provides a testing methodology for theoretical hypotheses which have been first formulated through introspection. Whether a linguist's theoretical position is "bottom-up" or "top-down", CL has shown itself to be a necessary element of the linguist's toolkit.

Regarding technology, nowadays, we should not understand CL without computation. Essentially, the adequate use of language technologies allows testing without the influence of the researcher's preconceptions (e.g., Juola, 2015). Textbooks in CL illustrate standard operating protocols for handling data and proper statistical analysis in both academic and industrial settings (e.g., Berber-Sardinha and Veirano, 2019; Cantos, 2013). In sum, computation is key to CL as it contributes to a more reliable and evidence-based analysis. Furthermore, it allows the handling of huge amount of text in a quick and replicable way. Thus, CL is to be framed within an interdisciplinary and integrated view of language research.

As for forensic linguistics, it is a fairly recent field, but it has evolved significantly over the last two decades. In the specific branch of forensic computational linguistics, tools from linguistics, corpus linguistics and computational linguistics are used to solve forensic issues. Thus, instead of considering forensic linguistics as a separate field, linguists in this area prefer to bring tested methods from different fields of linguistics as a science to the forensic setting. Thus, it can be stated that forensic computational linguistics was developed out of linguistic theory and computational linguistics.

In this field, it is especially important for corpus linguists that they follow standard CL procedures when they work in the forensic setting, promoting linguistics as a forensic science. For instance, word frequency can be presented as a raw count, but this is not as useful as the "relative" or "normalized frequency" of the word in relation to the entire word count of the corpus. When the relative frequency is calculated, corpora of different sizes can be compared. Thus, raw counts are hardly ever used in CL, since texts are almost always of different sizes. Likewise, raw counts should not be used in the forensic setting in the comparison of texts of different sizes.

Interestingly, in order to improve the accuracy of an automated approach, a semi-automatic computer-assisted approach is desirable. The semi-automatic or computer-assisted approach, using human experts to correct any errors of automatic annotation, is especially recommended when there is a justification based on the use for which the corpus is designed, such as forensic uses. Thus, in this field it is highly recommended to apply regular procedures like checking to make sure the software tagged properly, not necessarily because the software is defective, but simply because even the best commercial POS-taggers have an error rate of 3-4% –industry wide standard (Jurafsky and Martin, 2021). In industrial uses of computational linguistics, using human experts to correct any errors of automatic annotation is standard practice. Likewise, this should be standard operating procedure in the forensic setting too.

Furthermore, in order for forensic linguistics to serve its purpose of providing linguistic evidence in court, the discipline requires a series of scientific standards, which makes it reliable and replicable. According to the Institute for Linguistic Evidence[2] paradigm (henceforth, ILE), standards for forensic computational linguistic methodology include that forensic linguistics provides an empirical analysis grounded in linguistic theory, and that it can be replicated (Chaski, 2001; 2012). Accordingly, Coulthard (1994) advocated for the use of corpus in forensic linguistics given the possibilities that the empirical exploration of corpora can provide in terms of evidence. He stated that "any improved methodology must depend, to a large extent, on the setting up and analyzing of corpora" (Coulthard, 1994: 40). Indeed, within the forensic computational linguistic paradigm, Chaski (2001) developed the first specific corpus for forensic authorship identification so that methods can be grounded in empirical analysis.

Another relevant issue is the importance of working on ground-truth data that are forensically feasible. "Ground-truth" data means data that we know what the correct answers are, so, for deception detection, we need data where we know which documents are true or false. When a method is tested on

---

[2] https://linguisticevidence.org/

ground-truth data, we can conduct validation testing and accurately report its error rate. In empirical research, validation testing is a technique that determines how well a procedure works, in specific conditions, on a dataset containing samples of known origin (Chaski, 2012). Thus, on a database of ground-truth data, the researcher is to apply a replicable analytical method to every text, as well as a cross-validation scheme, most typically by building a statistical or an ML model. Last, the error rate is to be computed from the mis-classifications in the analysis.

Within this research paradigm, in the present work an example of forensic computational linguistics in the framework of text typing will be presented, with some approaches attempting to answer the question "Is this truthful or false?" It is worth noting that computer-assisted methods in other corners like author identification are much more consolidated worldwide and generally admitted in court, like Chaski's SynAID (2001; 2013), as compared to computer-assisted deception detection, which is not often used for veracity assessment in the legal setting.

## 2.3.2 Types of data in deception detection

As stated by Markowitz and Hancock (2019), context has proved to be an important aspect in research and affects the relation between lying and language. These authors have developed a model called the Contextual organization of Language and Deception (CoLD), which provides a framework

25

including some crucial aspects of context for any deceptive communication. In this regard, it is worth noting that much has been discussed about the importance of deception in spontaneously produced language. Laboratory-produced lies have been criticized in forensic literature for not being very reliable (e.g., Bull et al., 2006), and Sporer, Manzanero, and Masip (2020) suggest that further research should involve retrospective studies in law enforcement settings, to study realistic responses with known outcomes.

Nonetheless, the strength of laboratory-produced data is the possibility for controlling variables and attributes so that the conclusions drawn are experimentally valid (Almela, 2021a). What remains constant during such an experiment are the participants and the topics on which they write, which allows the researcher to avoid confounding intervening variables and to focus on deception in opinions and memories as the only plausible causal factor. Put another way, providing that some variation is observed regarding the dependent variables analyzed, this scientific control will allow the researcher(s) to assure that the participants' situations were identical until they were asked to lie, and so the potentially new outcome may be attributed to the independent variable. The usefulness of this kind of corpus has indeed been proved in the forensic context, as shown in studies like Fitzpatrick and Bachenko (2013).

In sum, in deception detection research there are two main types of data: (1) low-stakes deception, in which no harm can be done (it is well-known that people lie in social situations without intending harm); and (2) high-stakes deception, where real-life damages are possible and likely. This distinction

26

must be considered when drawing conclusions in computer-assisted deception detection research.

Regarding everyday lies, Burgoon, Buller and Woodall (1996) argue that deceivers tend to adapt their strategy during an interaction on the basis of the success of their deception. The communication modalities most suitable for this adaptation process are face-to-face oral interaction and synchronous computer-mediated communication (CMC). In distance modalities such as asynchronous CMC or mail correspondence, immediate feedback is not so often available for the deceiver, thus the adaptation of their strategy is not so straightforward. In this respect, DePaulo et al. (1996) deem this kind of lying as an intrinsic part of everyday life, and address the categorization of lying as follows: outright (total falsehoods), exaggerated (overstated facts and impressions), and subtle lies (evasions, omissions, and literal truths). A high percentage of lying occurs in social contexts and is low-consequence; as Picornell (2012: 19) puts it, in the event of detection "the consequences are little more than temporary slight embarrassment".

Everyday lies are contrasted with serious deception occurring in forensic contexts, which may lead to far-reaching consequences. In these situations, uncovering the full truth is essential for the clearing up of criminal and civil cases. Traditionally, a cue to deception considered sufficiently reliable in forensic investigations is nervousness or anxiety. An interrogated suspect displaying anxious behavior is deemed likely to have something to hide. Nevertheless, some researchers have recently advanced that anxiety is not

27

always an unequivocal symptom of deception. Specifically, Bull et al. (2006) insist that nervousness often arises from the stressful situation of a police interview. Most people are not used to police interrogations, and the mere fact of becoming a suspect makes them feel rather awkward. The authors also state that sometimes police officers behave in an accusatory way, which may intimidate the interviewees and lead to a leakage in behavior, independent of the truth value of the statement, which is often interpreted erroneously.

In fact, it is often claimed that some guilty suspects are able to manage their arousal and uneasiness far better than innocent ones, owing to the fact that they have become highly experienced in police interviews. As stated by Mann, Vrij and Bull (2002: 372),

> [d]ue to the large differences in people's attitudes, the content and consequences of their lies, their experience, and their ability to lie, there is never likely to be a less vague indicator than this [a change from normal behavior within a particular individual].

In their study on high-stakes deception, the authors indeed highlight the basic differences in non-verbal behavior during deceptive interactions between individuals. Furthermore, their findings reveal that anxiety does not play such a key role in deception as generally believed. This is monitored, among other non-verbal signs, through eye blinking, an increase of which had been previously associated with nervousness and anxiety. These researchers find that suspects blink less when lying, which they explain on the grounds of cognitive load. Significantly enough, deceivers also make longer pauses, which is attributed to the same reason by the researchers.

28

Both in common law and in civil law jurisdictions, the practice of deception is duly punished; accordingly, deceit is a tort and often a crime. The case *Derry v Peek*[3] is often quoted in the study of deceit within common law, since it is the first time deceit is defined, despite the fact that there was no sufficient evidence to confirm that deceit really occurred (Burdick, 1905: 373):

> The ground upon which an alleged belief was founded is a most important test of its reality… if I thought that a person making a false statement had shut his eyes to the facts, or purposely abstained from inquiring into them, I should hold that honest belief was absent…

In this regard, the intention to deceive the addressee is worth commenting on. In criminal law, intention or purpose is one of the four general types of *mens rea*[4] or the required mental state necessary to constitute a conventional as opposed to a strict liability crime, and it is said that it "requires a finding that the defendant has as a conscious objective to commit the act or result proscribed by the crime" (Strader, 2002: 9). The Spanish equivalent of this concept is *dolo* –literally, intention. This is certainly applicable to deceit within the forensic context, as shown in Green (as cited in Mahon, 2015: 21), who advances that lying is neither necessary nor sufficient for perjury in common law, since if a person, under oath to testify, declare, depose, or certify truly, before a competent officer, willfully makes an untruthful statement without the

---

[3] (1889) 14 App Cas 337

[4] Strader (2002) arranges the four types of *mens rea* from the most difficult to the least difficult to prove: intention or purpose, knowledge, recklessness, and negligence.

intention that any other person believe it to be true, the person is not lying, but they are considered to have committed perjury –a federal crime consisting of deliberately giving false, incomplete or inaccurate information. On the contrary, providing that a person is under oath and willfully makes an allegedly untruthful statement with the intention that it is believed to be true, and the statement happens to be so, the person has not committed perjury.

Of interest, there is an exception to the commitment to tell only the whole truth in trials: in modern legal systems, no person is compelled to testify against themselves. In the context of Anglo-American common law, this originated in medieval England and Wales. This legal system has since then been in charge of the provision to individuals with the means to protect themselves from self-incrimination, guaranteeing fundamental fairness, justice, and liberty by means of the due process (Levy, 1969). The well-known Fifth Amendment to the United States Constitution enshrines the above-mentioned privilege against self-incrimination and the right to silence: "No person [...] shall be compelled in any criminal case to be a witness against himself, nor be deprived of life, liberty, or property, without due process of law."[5] This is crystallized in the Miranda warning, which is given by police in the United States to criminal suspects in police custody and during custodial interrogations. The rest of the countries deriving their laws as an extension of the English Common Law have equivalent rights, although some of them have their own peculiarities. Most

---

[5] Bill of Rights from Cornell University Law School, publicly available at http://www.law.cornell.edu/constitution/fifth_amendment

notably, the English Criminal Justice and Public Order Act 1994 amended the right to silence by allowing the jury to draw inferences in the event of a suspect providing an explanation after having refused to do so during custodial interrogation. Accordingly, although the jury is also free to not make such an inference, law supports their assumption of a defendant's alleged fabrication. This amendment has been rejected outright by most common law jurisdictions, on the grounds that an innocent person may also have a reason for not speaking freely to investigating police (Bagaric, 1997). However, in these jurisdictions a testifying defendant is sworn to tell the truth under oath and pain of perjury.

As regards civil law jurisdictions, these guarantees are taken a step forward. In the particular case of Spain, Article 24 of the Spanish Constitution enshrines the right to effective protection of the court –*tutela judicial efectiva*–, which is a similar concept to the due process in common law. Two fundamental rights are specified in the second section of this article: the privilege against self-incrimination and the right not to plead guilty. According to Aparicio (2010), this has often been interpreted as having a positive side embodied in the so-called "right to lie". The author explains that this right is not explicitly acknowledged in Spanish legislation, but the aforementioned rights were established, as in common law, so as to create a safety net which prevents others from entering the private sphere of people when detrimental consequences may be derived for fundamental rights, which is the case when a person is involved in criminal proceedings. However, the Spanish Constitutional Court states that the defendant is not legally compelled to tell the

31

truth, hence the relinquishment by the State to punish this behavior (Ríos, 2019). At this point, the main difference from common law jurisdictions is that a defendant does not swear an oath and is not technically a witness; thus, if they lie, they are not committing perjury.

Closely related to this different treatment of the defendant's statement is the concept of the plea, which is one of the major differences between both legal systems. In common law, a defendant may be sentenced immediately after their guilty plea, whereas civil law jurisdictions generally lack this concept. A confession by the defendant is treated like any other piece of evidence. Even if they provide a full confession, the trial is not prevented from occurring (Etienne, 2005). Probably due to the considerable relevance of the defendant's testimony and the checking of its veracity in common law jurisdictions, research on high-stakes deception is much more developed than in civil law tradition countries such as Spain, whose legal system cannot punish the defendant for lying if the lies have been told in the exercise of the privilege against self-incrimination.

There are some particular cases in which deception is considered to display special characteristics. For instance, children are usually lacking in credibility due to their overactive imagination (Bull, 1997), and their production of lies is usually studied apart. Furthermore, pathological lying has been deemed a special form of deception. A working definition of this phenomenon is provided by Healy and Healy (1969: 1):

Pathological lying is falsification entirely disproportionate to any discernible end in view, engaged in by a person who, at the time of observation, cannot definitively be declared insane, feebleminded, or epileptic. Such lying rarely, if ever, centers about an event; although exhibited in very occasional cases for a short time, it manifests itself most frequently by far over a period of years, or even a lifetime. It represents a trait rather than an episode.

Thus, this type of deception is characterized by a medical record of frequent lying for no apparent reason.

According to Hausman (2003), most scholarly literature references agree that pathological lying should be differentiated from other psychiatric conditions associated with different forms of deception. The most representative ones are psychopathy (Hare et al., 1989), antisocial personality disorder or ASPD (Ford, 1999), obsessive-compulsive disorder or OCD (Dike, 2008), narcissistic personality disorder or NPD (DSM IV-TR, 2000), histrionic personality disorder or HPD (DSM IV-TR, 2000), borderline personality disorder or BPD (Böhm and Steller, 2008), factitious or Münchausen disorder (Feldman, Ford and Reinhold, 1993), and Ganser syndrome (Carney et al., 1987). The particular case of confabulation is also worthy of attention. It is defined as a condition where patients try to plug memory gaps generated by organically derived amnesia with confabulated material (Dalla Barba, 1993). The special features of mental patients with these disorders make research on their untruthful speech a separate branch of study. For instance, ordinary lies are told with the intention to avoid punishment or to obtain an external benefit;

33

on the contrary, pathological lying is rather purposeless and sometimes even self-incriminating.

### 2.3.3 The role of linguistic variables in computer-assisted deception analysis

As has been seen, deception detection can play a role in the investigation of different security issues, civil cases, and even some types of crimes. The adoption of totally automated deception detection methods and mixed machine-human methods entail some basic stages: choosing an appropriate linguistic level, properly codifying the variables of analysis, engaging in statistical analysis, and conducting validation testing.

As stated in Almela (2021a), this kind of analyses can make use of variables from different linguistic levels, namely the phonemic, morphemic, lexical, syntactic, semantic, and pragmatic. As Chaski (2012) puts it, forensic methods dealing with written data have focused on analytical units at the character, word, sentence, and text levels. Specifically, some studies like Zhou et al. (2004) present automated methods for deception detection operating at the character level, whose analytical units include, among others, single characters, punctuation marks, or character-level n-grams (units of adjacent characters). At the word level, analytical units can be word-level n-grams (e.g., Mihalcea and Strapparava, 2009), lexical semantics (e.g., Newman et al., 2003), and vocabulary richness (e.g., Almela, Alcaraz-Mármol and Cantos, 2015).

34

Sentence-level analytical units can include part-of-speech (POS) tags (e.g., Fornaciari and Poesio, 2013), sentence type (e.g., Feng, Banerjee and Choi, 2012), average sentence length (e.g., Pérez-Rosas and Mihalcea, 2015), and average number of clauses per utterance (e.g., Yancheva and Rudzicz, 2013). At the text level, analytical units can include text length (e.g., Almela, Valencia-García and Cantos, 2013) and discourse strategies (e.g., Rubin and Vashchilko, 2012), to name but a few. The easiest patterns to detect by machines are character and word level features. On the contrary, at other linguistic levels automatic pattern detection is harder, especially with forensic data, as they are often messy. For instance, sentence level features can be extracted automatically, but most parsers require human revision of the output to ensure the accuracy of the analysis.

In their meta-analysis of computer-assisted deception detection, Hauch et al. (2015) explored 44 studies and a set of 79 cues which seemed initially consistent across previous literature. The main metric calculated for their assessment was Cohen's (1988) effect size $d$, firstly used for deception detection analysis by DePaulo et al. (2003: 89), and defined by the authors as follows:

> The effect size computed for each behavioral difference was $d$, defined as the mean for the deceptive condition (i.e., the lies) minus the mean for the truthful condition (i.e., the truths), divided by the mean of the standard deviations for the truths and the lies.

Accordingly, positive $d$s indicate that the behavior occurred more often during deception than truth, whereas negative $d$s indicate the opposite. Hauch et al. (2015) revealed small to moderate effect sizes for cues indicative of deceit. Most importantly, these effects were influenced by moderators, such as interaction type and production mode, and specific context. Despite some inconsistencies, the authors reported some common conclusions for the poll of studies reviewed: in broad terms, liars experienced greater cognitive load than truth-tellers, using fewer words related to cognitive processes, they used more negative emotion words, detached themselves from the events narrated, and used fewer sensory-perceptual words. Nonetheless, words expressing uncertainty were found indicative neither of deception nor of truth. All in all, the results varied across the studies according to event type, involvement, intensity of interaction, and motivation, among other variables.

As for the description and explanation of the most significant methodologies, the most outstanding tools for automated deception detection are presented below. The first group is aimed at the automatic extraction of linguistic features for different purposes, whereas the second group includes software specifically developed for the computational classification of written statements as true or false.

At the basis of content analysis or of any text classification tasks is Deese's argument (1965) that common meaning in communication is, to a considerable extent, determined by the existence of a commonality of associative structures in different people; in other words, shared meanings are needed in a linguistic community for communication to take place. These meanings have proved to crystallize in recurrent patterns in language, and content analysis software is precisely aimed at their recognition. In this regard, Almela (2021a: 4) states that

> [o]ne of the earliest attempts at automated content analysis was the General Inquirer (Stone et al., 1962; Stone et al., 1966), and some years later Knapp, Hart and Dennis (1974) assessed several linguistic cues using TEXAN, a computer system that analyzed word frequencies by keypunching the words to map them to different lexical categories, with the main purpose of differentiating truths from lies in the written medium.

Interestingly, Deese (1969) advanced a psychological semantic theory in the context of content analysis, certainly needed for the understanding of the method not as a mere classification of the lexis contained in a given text, but as a scientific tool that involves a psychological interpretation of semantic processes. The author insists that content analysis attempts to discover a portion of the themes of a text determined by the psychological or social aims of the analysis and by the need for statistical treatment, enabling systematic analysis of linguistic data through conceptual categories. Accordingly, the definition of analytical constructs and linguistic foundations serving as scaffolding for content analysis software must not be disregarded, as they may contribute to the robust implementation of the method.

In the last two decades, some more modern content analysis approaches were developed in research contexts on similar grounds, outstandingly Linguistic Inquiry and Word Count, or LIWC (Pennebaker, Francis and Booth, 2001). Although both systems relate linguistic text to other categories of cognition, one important difference between LIWC and the General Inquirer is that LIWC focuses on the word as the unit of analysis, while the General Inquirer was based on the sentence. Shortly after the release of the General Inquirer, Goldhamer (1969) explained the wide variety of items that their software could search for, namely: the beginning of the sentence where the node word was contained; other words in the context; tags assigned to other words; sentence-level identification; current statistics on the sentence and document; document-level identification; and tags assigned to previous sentence.

Regarding LIWC, the categories used in the original version of the software were related to standard linguistic processes, psychological processes, relativity, and personal matters; a detailed description of the individual categories can be found in Pennebaker and Graybeal (2001). It has been also adapted and translated into more than ten languages, including Spanish (Ramírez-Esparza et al., 2007), as will be seen in Chapter 4. In sum, it provides a tool for studying the emotional, cognitive, and structural components contained in language on a word-by-word basis, working out the percentage of words which fall into those categories. Newman et al. (2003) were the first researchers to apply this system to deception detection, yielding above-chance accuracy of classifications for different types of lies. Over the last few years, it has been widely used in fields like forensic linguistics (e.g., Mihalcea and Strapparava, 2009; Skillicorn and Lamb, 2013), sentiment analysis (e.g., Salas-Zárate et al., 2014), and psycholinguistics (e.g., Almela et al., 2019).

Some other automatic text classification tools have been developed beyond word frequency analysis, such as CohMetrix (Graesser et al., 2004; McNamara, et al., 2014). It analyzes cohesion relations, taking into account meaning and context in which words or phrases occur in texts. Bedwell et al. (2011) were the first researchers to apply it to deception detection.

Regarding software specifically developed for linguistic deception detection is presented, one of the most famous methods for deception detection is Scientific Content Analysis (SCAN). It was developed by Sapir (1987), a polygraph examiner, and methods based on it are generally known as Statement Analysis. Most of the literature published on this type of analysis is merely descriptive (e.g., Lesce, 1990; McClish, 2001), although it was automated with reported accuracy results of 71% by Fitzpatrick and Bachenko (2013). However, as stated by Fitzpatrick, Bachenko and Fornaciari (2015), SCAN and other statement analysis systems have been mainly used and taught by practitioners manually, with several studies having examined SCAN with suggestive but inconsistent results (e.g. Adams and Jarvis, 2006; Kang and Lee, 2014).

Some other computational tools have been specifically developed for deception detection, such as Agent99Analyzer (Fuller et al., 2006), created to extract linguistic cues to deception from texts and videos, iSkim (Zhou, Booker and Zhang, 2002), or CueCal (Zhou et al., 2004). A somewhat different detection deception software is ADAM, or Automated Deception Analysis Machine (Derrick et al., 2012), which focuses on editing processes like backspace or spacebar while typing messages, as well as measuring response latencies. The main methodological drawback of this approach seems to be that it requires a keystroke analyzer being on the interviewee's machine, which can be seen as intrusion of privacy.

Remarkably, most previous studies in computerized deception detection have relied exclusively on shallow lexico-syntactic patterns. However, Feng et al. (2012) were the first researchers to explore syntactic stylometry. Over four different datasets including service reviews and essays on different topics, the authors explore features derived from Phrase Structure Grammar (PSG) parse trees, showing that they consistently improve the detection rate over several baselines that are based only on lexical features. Most relevantly, within the four datasets examined, they apply their method to Ott et al.'s (2011) corpus from TripAdvisor, improving the classification results obtained by its collectors by reaching around 91% accuracy.

In this line of linguistic sophistication, a valuable contribution to linguistic deception detection has been made by Witness Statement Evaluation Research (WISER), one of the tools provided by ALIAS Technology[6], a company which offers forensic linguistics consulting to attorneys, law enforcement, human resources, and security teams. ALIAS WISER is a project using automated text analysis and statistical classifiers to determine the best protocol for computational classification of true and false statements in the

---

[6] https://aliastechnology.com/

forensic-investigative setting. Chaski et al. (2015) tested this text analysis tool, based on ALIAS's module Text Analysis Toolkit Toward Linguistic Evidence Research (TATTLER). It combines linguistic analysis at the phonological, syntactic, and lexico-semantic levels, described in detail in Chapter 5. Of interest, ALIAS WISER yielded substantially different results depending on the nature of the dataset, as about 70% of the texts in the laboratory dataset were correctly identified using leave-one-out cross-validation (Almela, 2021b; Chaski, in press), while the rate reached more than 92% for high-stakes deception (Chaski, 2021; Chaski et al., 2014), which can be considered as the most successful rate published to date. Indeed, this brings to light the contrast provided to lies told in a low-stakes, laboratory setting by the ones told in a police investigation. All in all, these studies show how TATTLER linguistic variables work better than text analysis tools used for different purposes, like LIWC or simplistic NLP models like Bag of Words (BoW). The latter is an approach popular among computer scientists working in text classification; the term Bag of Words was invented by Harris (1954) and developed by Salton and McGill (1983), and in this conception of language each text is seen as a list of words and their frequencies without regard to any morphosyntax or semantics.

As stated above, context has proved to affect the relation between lying and language (e.g., Almela, Valencia-García and Cantos, 2012). Thus, the development of software designed for specific contextual frameworks is especially valuable in deception detection. An outstanding example of contextualized analysis of deception is VeriPol (Quijano-Sánchez et al., 2018), a model for the detection of false robbery reports in Spanish based only on their text. This tool, developed in collaboration with the Spanish National Police and the Ministry of the Interior, combines NLP and ML methods in a decision support system that provides police officers the probability that a given report is false. The impact of this tool was tested by means of an on-the-field pilot study that took place in 10 Spanish Police Departments in 2017, specifically on a corpus of 588 false robbery reports and 534 truthful robbery reports, which is great practice, as explained above on the use of ground-truth data. For the analysis, the authors applied feature selection techniques in their approaches, using model variables like POS tags, document statistics (e.g., number of tokens, lemmata, and sentences within a document), and unigram lemmata for the performance of ML and statistical classification techniques. They concluded that, in general, the more details provided in the report, the more likely it is to be truthful. Empirical results show that it is extremely effective in discriminating between false and true reports with a success rate of more than 91%, improving by more than 15% the accuracy of human expert police officers on the same dataset. The pilot study was so successful that nowadays it is officially used in all the National Police offices in Spain.

This is indeed significant, as despite the fact that computer-assisted deception detection is not generally considered in Spanish courts, it is proved that investigative settings may benefit from its assistance. Indeed, the differences between the situation of forensic linguistics in English- and Spanish-speaking countries are worth noting at this point. As Bull et al. (2006)

explain, there is an ever-growing respect between British police, criminal psychologists and linguists, probably because of the well-established tradition of these disciplines in English-speaking countries. However, in countries like Spain these areas do not have such a long tradition, hence the difficulty when it comes to securing comprehensive assistance to conduct realistic lie detection studies in languages other than English.

All in all, computer-assisted detection deception in both the WISER and VeriPol studies demonstrate that detection is possible with over 90% accuracy, with high-stakes ground-truth data.

# CHAPTER 3. Research methodology

## 3.1 Contextualizing the studies

In this chapter, the methodology of the two empirical studies reported in Chapter 4 and Chapter 5 is presented, whose aim is to explore the linguistic cues to deception in written language using computational tools such as LIWC, WordSmith, and ALIAS WISER. After the automated text analysis, statistical classifiers are used to determine the best protocol for computational classification of true and false statements. The tools have been tested on ground-truth data, which involves the use of data where the researcher knows what the correct answers are, as only with ground-truth data the researcher can accurately report its error rate. Specifically, in previous work, the results showed a remarkable difference between the experimental data, in which students were asked to write true and false narratives, and high-stakes data, actual statements from real criminal investigations with non-linguistic evidence of their veracity or falsehood (e.g., Chaski et al., 2015). This result demonstrates that there is a real difference between lies told in an experimental setting (or "laboratory-produced") and lies told in a police investigation (what is known as "high-stakes deception").

The experimental dataset comprises subcorpora in two languages: English and Spanish. The former was collected by Mihalcea and Strapparava (2009), and the latter was collected by Almela et al. (2013) and made public in Almela

(2021a). These corpora do not contain spontaneously produced language, but the Hawthorne effect was minimized by not explicitly telling the participants the ultimate aim of the study. As for the high-stakes dataset in English, it comprises 35 witness statements previously analyzed in Chaski et al. (2015) and Picornell (2013), which provides a solid basis for comparison.

For the sake of clarity, Table 3.1 provides a summary of the classification techniques applied to the corpora:

| Data | Aim | Methodology | Input |
|------|-----|-------------|-------|
| Low-stakes datasets (English and Spanish) | Cross-linguistic comparison (English vs Spanish) | Binary logistic regression and DFA (IBM SPSS) | LIWC categories (LIWC2001) |
| | | | Stylometric features (WordSmith) |
| Low-stakes datasets and high-stakes dataset (English) | Intralingual comparison (low stakes vs high stakes) | DFA (IBM SPSS) | WISER (ALIAS Technology) |

Table 3.1 Methodologies and techniques used in the data analysis

Almela et al. (2012) predates the first experiment reported here. It is worth noting that this test was first conducted in fulfillment of the present author's requirements as a doctoral candidate, but only part of it has been published for the scientific community so far, namely automatic classification experiments in Spanish (Almela et al., 2013; Almela, 2021a). As stated above, Almela et al. (2013) conducted a classification experiment testing the Spanish version of LIWC2001 (Ramírez-Esparza et al., 2007) to classify a dataset similar to that of Mihalcea and Strapparava (2009), trained and tested with a Support Vector Machine classifier using the four dimensions of LIWC separately (standard linguistic dimensions, psychological constructs, general descriptors, and personal concerns), and afterwards with the possible combinations of the four dimensions. The authors showed the high performance of the automatic classifier in Spanish written texts through the experiments, conducted on three datasets, checking the discriminant power of the variables as to their truth condition, being the two first dimensions, linguistic and psychological processes, the most relevant ones. Specifically, the best performing combinations across all LIWC tests and topics was an F-measure of 84.5% using the combination of all four categories on the good friend topic. For comparison with the other LIWC studies that use F-measure, Ott et al.'s (2011) highest F-measure was 76.9% using the LIWC features alone on the more lexically constrained hotel reviews, and Fornaciari and Poesio's (2013) was 79.6%. Almela et al. (2013) and Almela (2021a) state that the higher performance on the good friend topic shows the strong dependence of the task on topic and attribute the better performance on this topic to the greater emotional involvement that narrators have in describing their best friend.

In this line of reasoning, the first study presented here is a subsequent experiment conducted on the same corpora, and adopting some of the suggestions for further research put forward in Almela (2021a). Interestingly, the novelty of this monograph is twofold:

(1) Study 1: A cross-linguistic study of deception in which the variables used to explore low-stakes deception in Spanish are contrasted to a comparable corpus in English.

(2) Study 2: An intralingual experiment (English) in which low-stakes data are contrasted to high-stakes data.

As mentioned above, the main area of research of the present monograph is the study of language by means of corpus-based and computational techniques. Nevertheless, like any interdisciplinary subject, the detection of deception in written language involves the combination of two or more academic fields in the pursuit of a common task, crossing traditional boundaries between linguistics, computation and psychology.

## 3.2 Method

The method addresses the different stages in the development of the present study. This section comprises three main parts: an introduction to the nature of the study, the corpora description, and the data analysis process.

### *3.2.1 Nature of the study*

The current study involves a combination of primary and secondary research. As Brown and Rodgers (2002) put it, primary research deals with original data, whereas secondary research is based on bibliographical resources such as scientific books and papers. The previous chapter, where the theoretical basis for this study is formed, provides a sample of secondary research. A piece of primary research may be found in Chapters 3, 4 and 5. Specifically, the present chapter offers detailed information about the development of the study.

Furthermore, the study may be classified as quasi-experimental. Quasi-experiments resemble quantitative and qualitative experiments, but they lack random assignment of groups or proper controls (Shadish et al., 2002). This feature has been seen as an inherent weakness, especially from the viewpoint of experimental purists in the natural sciences. However, this is a very useful design for measuring social variables, since it is not always possible to accomplish a purely random allocation of groups when dealing with human subjects. Thus, the present research takes advantage of the possibilities of this experimental design, by comparing two groups of participants under similar circumstances. As explained below, an inter-group comparison has been drawn, delving into the similarities and differences of the linguistic profiling of deception in written communication across languages. In addition, an intra-group assessment has been undertaken in order to explore differences across topics, using the truthful statements as the control subcorpus against which the untruthful data set is compared. Due to the quasi-experimental nature of the study, the intention is not to generalize the inferences drawn from the data analysis, but they are to be treated provisionally.

The nature of the linguistic data of the corpora is also worth commenting on. As mentioned in Chapter 2, much has been discussed about the importance of deception in language being naturally produced. Laboratory-produced lies have been criticized in forensic literature for not being very reliable:

> A major criticism of almost all published studies involving professionals is that the video clips shown to them have not been of people lying in real-life, high stakes situations (but usually of students lying for the purposes of the experiment) (Bull et al., 2006: 77).

Similarly, Miller and Stiff (1993) question the value of applying laboratory research results to field settings, and Sporer (1997) suggests that further research should involve retrospective studies in law enforcement settings, to study realistic responses with known outcomes. Nevertheless, it presents some practical difficulties. First of all, the veracity or deception of the narratives has to be previously determined (non-linguistic evidence), and this is not always an easy task. Generally speaking, the accounts are not to be taken as truthful or untruthful blocks of information, but rather as sets of truthful and untruthful statements. Thus, their categorization becomes a complex task. On the contrary, this problem does not exist in a laboratory-controlled set of data, where the corresponding accounts are untruthful as a whole.

One of the major criticisms of those studies not dealing with real-life situations is the participants' absence of anxiety. This emotion is considered to arise from the guilt experienced by an offender making a false statement, as well as from the possible consequences of being caught lying. Obviously, in a laboratory-controlled situation this element is absent, or minimized at best. However, this may be considered to be not so negative, since, as Bull et al. (2006: 79) put it, one of the main beliefs falsely associated with deceivers is that "people who look nervous are liars (when they are probably just socially anxious or introverted)". This anxiety is often provoked by police interviewers behaving in an accusatory way, which may be transmitted to interviewees, resulting in an increase in their nervousness, whether lying or telling the truth. In this way, the language of deception in an experimental corpus is not spoilt by a pressing situation. Furthermore, professional and recidivist liars do not experience anxiety when deceiving, so it has been deemed interesting to neutralize this factor. In addition, it especially influences spontaneously produced oral language, where the suspects do not have enough time to plan and organize their speech; however, this is not always the case with written statements, since the amount of time available is usually enough to carefully plan the language and thus to control the initial anxiety.

On the other hand, the strength of laboratory-produced data is the possibility for controlling variables and attributes so that the conclusions drawn are valid. What remains constant during this experiment are the participants and the topics on which they write, which allows the researcher to avoid confounding variables and to focus on deception in opinions and memories as the only plausible causal factor. Put another way, providing that some variation is observed regarding the dependent variables analyzed, this scientific control will allow the present author to assure that the participants' situations were identical until they were asked to lie, and so the potentially new outcome may be attributed to the independent variable. The usefulness of this kind of corpus has indeed been proved in the forensic context, as shown in Chapter 2 (e.g. Fitzpatrick and Bachenko, 2010). Apart from research on verbal cues to deception, some tools for detecting deception on a physiological basis rely on "on-purpose lying". Such is the case of the functioning of a polygraph, which is adjusted by means of some preliminary questions in which the subject is deliberately asked to lie (Arce and Fariña, 2006). Specifically, the subject is usually asked to choose from any two numbers, for instance 1 and 6. They must then try to deny this selection when offered between 1 and 10. After the responses, the subject is informed that a change has been observed with respect to the other numbers, and is warned to be honest, otherwise their deceiving will be detected (Bradley and Janisse, 1981). This application in a realistic setting shows the validity of on-purpose lying.

Last but not least, the differences between the situation of forensic linguistics in English-speaking countries and Spanish-speaking countries are worth noting. As Bull et al. (2006) assure, there is an ever-growing respect between British police, criminal psychologists and linguists, probably because of the long tradition of these disciplines in English-speaking countries. However, in countries like Spain these areas are in their infancy, hence the difficulty when it comes to securing comprehensive assistance to conduct realistic lie detection studies in Spanish.

### 3.2.2 Corpora

The instruments used in the present study can be classified as follows: (1) low-stakes (English/Spanish); (2) high-stakes (English).

It is worth noting that, although the language in the corpus object of study has not been produced in a realistic setting, medium motivation is involved in the present study, as suggested by Hancock et al. (2010) and Ott et al. (2011). During the collection of both datasets, the participants were told that they had to make sure they were able to convince the readers about the topics on which they were lying. In addition, incentives were offered to increase external validity in both cases. The incentive provided by Mihalcea and Strapparava (2009) was monetary, since the participants were Amazon Mechanical Turk workers. Moreover, the requesters had the option to reject the results submitted by the workers, which would reflect on their reputation, hence the strengthening of their motivation. As regards the data set in Spanish, the students participating in the project were awarded extra credit which might improve the final grade of the course.

Furthermore, the Hawthorne effect (McCarney et al., 2007) was minimized by not explicitly telling the subjects the ultimate aim of the research, since they might have modified the behavior experimentally measured on the basis of their awareness.

The low-stakes corpus used for English was collected by Mihalcea and Strapparava (2009)[7]. Their sample comprised 100 participants whose contributions were gathered through Amazon Mechanical Turk (MTurk)[8], one of the suites of Amazon Web Services. It is a crowdsourcing Internet marketplace that allows computer programmers and researchers in general to coordinate the use of human intelligence to perform tasks that computers are unable to perform. The requesters can post Human Intelligence Tasks (HITs) to be fulfilled by workers. Its reliability as a source of data has been assessed in previous research (Snow et al., 2008). All the participants were native speakers of English, but no information is provided concerning either their variety of English or their age or sex. In order to offer a direct comparison with the existing set of data for English, the design of the Spanish corpus was similar, as commented on below.

For the design of the questionnaire, the authors focused on three different topics: opinions on abortion, opinions on the death penalty, and feelings about a good friend. For the first two topics, the authors provided instructions that asked the contributors to imagine they were taking part in a debate, and had 10-15 minutes to express their opinion about the topic. First, they were asked to prepare a brief speech expressing their true opinion on the topic. Next, they were asked to prepare a second brief speech expressing the opposite of their

---

[7] The researchers kindly accepted to share their corpus for the purposes of the present study during the period I spent as a visiting scholar at Fondazione Bruno Kessler in Trento (Italy).

[8] Service available at https://www.mturk.com

opinion, thus lying about their true beliefs. Participants were told that the content of the messages needed to be unambiguously truthful or deceptive, and, in both cases, the guidelines asked for at least 4-5 sentences in as much detail as possible. For the other topic, the contributors were first asked to think about a good friend of theirs, including facts and anecdotes considered relevant to their relationship. Thus, in this case, they were asked to tell the truth about how they felt. Next, they were asked to think about a person who they disliked, and describe them as if they were good friends. In this second case, they had to lie about their feelings toward that person. As before, the guidelines asked for at least 4-5 detailed sentences.

They collected 100 true and 100 concocted statements for each topic, making a total of 600 contributions, with an average of 85 words per statement and a total of 51,204 words. Each verbal sample was entered into a separate text file; they made a manual verification of the contributions and misspellings were corrected. Table 3.2 provides a sample of this corpus.

| TRUTH | LIE |
|---|---|
| ABORTION ||
| I am against abortion. I feel that to get an abortion done is a crime equivalent to murder. You are killing an unborn child and taking away his chance of coming into this world. The innocent soul to whom God has given the chance to come in human form is being deprived of this golden opportunity. Spirituality says that it is only in human form that one can realize oneself to be a soul and know God. | I think abortion is one's own personal decision and nobody should interfere in that. People must be allowed to decide for themselves whether they want to have the child or not. There can be several reasons why the person would want to abort the child. So only the parents know better whether it's the right time for them or not, they will be able to support the child or not, etc, etc. |
| DEATH PENALTY ||
| I believe the death penalty should be abolished. As a country that was founded on Christian principles, this is one area of the law that has strayed far off the path. God should be the only giver of life and death. To end someone's life for any reason is sinful. It is just and right to punish those who commit crimes and keep them segregated from society for the safety of others. | The death penalty should stand as it is. It is a necessary part of our criminal justice system. There are many criminals who would recidivate if given the chance and therefore cannot be put back into society. However, for those who commit the most heinous of crimes, it is not feasible in terms of space or finances to keep them in prison for their entire lives. Our prisons would be filled to the max in no time. |
| FRIEND ||
| My best friend is so warm and inviting. | This girl is sweet but doesn't want you to |

| The first time I met her I felt like I had known her forever. I told her my life story, that's how comfortable I felt talking to her. She has the nicest smile and the funniest laugh! She has been there for me during good times and bad...she held my heart when it was broken when my son died and then again when I found out I had cancer. | know it! She has a huge smile, I wish she would use it more. We hang out and have fun together. My life is better for having known her. |
|---|---|

Table 3.2 Sample of truthful and untruthful statements in English (Mihalcea and Strapparava, 2009)

The design of the questionnaire for the compilation of the corpus was similar to the one described in the previous section for English (Mihalcea and Strapparava, 2009). Thus, the sample also comprised 100 participants and 600 contributions. All of them were university students, native speakers of Castilian or Peninsular Spanish. Specifically, the task was assigned as an exercise for extra credit, and sent back via e-mail. Personal information such as age and sex has not been taken into account, since it has been considered irrelevant to the present analysis.

It focused on three different topics: opinions on homosexual adoption, opinions on bullfighting, and feelings about a good friend. The first two topics (homosexual adoption and bullfighting) were controversial and sensitive subjects, which cause people to entertain a personal opinion on them. The participants were first asked to prepare a brief text expressing their true opinion on the topic. Next, they were asked to concoct a second brief text expressing the opposite of their opinion, thus lying about their true beliefs. In both cases, the guidelines asked for at least 4-5 sentences in as much detail as possible. As for the third topic, the contributors were asked to think about a good friend of theirs, including facts and anecdotes considered relevant to their relationship. That topic was selected so as to offer a counterpart to the previous ones, since they entailed less emotional involvement. Thus, they were asked to tell the truth about how they felt. Next, they were asked to think about a person they disliked, and describe them as if they were their best friend, lying about their feelings. As before, the guidelines asked for at least 4-5 detailed sentences. It is worth noting that time restrictions were not imposed for either language.

In line with the English corpus, 600 contributions were collected –100 true and 100 false statements for each topic–, with an average of 94 words per statement and a total of 56,882 words. A manual verification of the quality of the contributions was made, and each verbal sample was entered into a separate text file, misspellings being corrected. Table 3.3 shows a sample of truthful and untruthful language for each of the three topics.

| TRUTHFUL | UNTRUTHFUL |
|---|---|
| HOMOSEXUAL ADOPTION | |
| Para mí no está clara la repercusión que tendría sobre los niños el hecho de que las parejas homosexuales adopten. Sería necesario un estudio previo de las posibles consecuencias o secuelas psicológicas, o de la ausencia de ellas, en el mejor de los casos. | La familia es y ha sido siempre la formada por un hombre y una mujer. No debemos cambiar esto, pues es un claro síntoma de la degeneración de la sociedad. Hemos de defender las tradiciones que llevan funcionando bien durante miles de años. |
| BULLFIGHTING | |
| Es una salvajada. Regodearse en el sufrimiento de un animal, disfrutar viendo cómo realiza sus últimos movimientos, agotado y herido. ¿Cómo puede ser un arte esto? Sin duda hay muchas personas que están familiarizadas con las corridas de toros. | Los espectáculos relacionados con los toros son una tradición antiquísima y un arte. Es más, los toros de lidia se pasan la vida al aire libre y son bien mimados por sus criadores, disfrutando así de una vida muchísimo mejor que la que se les ofrece a los animales de granja. |
| FRIEND | |
| Cuando conocí a José María pensé que era uno más, que incluso no nos podríamos llevar bien. Qué equivocación más grande, ¡y qué afortunada! Es hoy uno de mis mejores amigos, que me | Sergio es un chaval inteligente, que sabe lo que quiere. Es realmente una buena persona, con la que puedes contar para todo. Su principal cualidad es su simpatía y amabilidad con todos, no importa que |

| encontré de casualidad en una de mis muchas andanzas por el mundo. | no te conozca de nada, siempre te da una oportunidad. |
| --- | --- |

Table 3.3 Sample of truthful and untruthful statements in Spanish

As explained in Almela (2021a), the dataset in Spanish was deposited by the present author in a publicly available database (see Fig. 3.1):

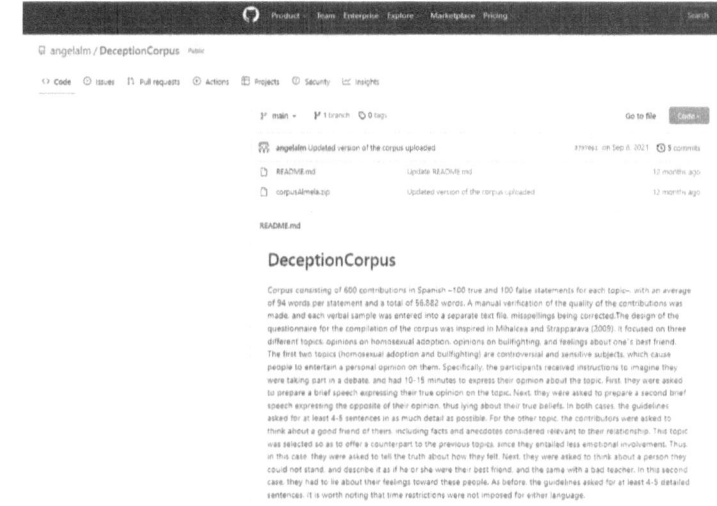

Figure 3.1 Screenshot of the Spanish corpus (Almela, 2021a), publicly available at

https://github.com/angelalm/DeceptionCorpus

As for the high-stakes dataset, it was kindly provided by Sgt. Larry Barksdale to the Institute for Linguistic Evidence. Specifically, as part of a normal investigative protocol, witnesses and suspects were asked to write a statement of what happened during the commission of a crime. The statements were determined to be essentially untruthful or essentially truthful based on corroborating evidence that became available during the investigation of the crimes. The subjects generated 7 untruthful witness statements and 28 truthful witness statements, for a total of 35 documents; Table 3.4 shows an example of both. This dataset has been previously analyzed in Chaski et al. (2015) and Picornell (2013) with different techniques.

| TRUTHFUL | UNTRUTHFUL |
|---|---|
| At approx 11:25am I went into our bedroom to get Timmy and put him in his carrier to go and pick up my 2 daughters from preschool.<br>When I picked him up I noticed that he was limp & unresponsive.<br>I then called 911 and laid Timmy down on the floor. I checked on Timmy around 11:10 – 15am and he was breathing and responding to my touch. He was awake and was fed at 9:00am. | I went to Vale about 7:00 – 7.30 I picked up Raquel and went to one of her friend's house. We left there and went down Braye Road and met Darren and Harvey we went with them for a while and went around the south quay.<br>Then we dropped them off at a cafe and picked up two more men. We went by Annabelle's house and I saw Annabelle and I told her I wanted to get rid of the men that were with me and she had something to do so she left. Raquel had |

| | went in the next apartment with Annabelle so I went and tried to drop off the men.<br><br>Right after I got in the car with the men I called my boyfriend and I wouldn't talk to him so he knew some thing [sic] was wrong. I drove a black male with a bigger nose about 6'4" dark brown eyes and a light man about 17 around the south quay until finally they said they wanted dropped off at Carteret School. |
| --- | --- |

Table 3.4 Sample of truthful and untruthful statements in the high-stakes dataset

### 3.2.3 Statistical analyses

The statistical techniques used to examine the questions raised above are advanced in this section. They were performed so as to assess the discriminant power of the different linguistic variables described in Chapter 4 and Chapter 5, retrieved by means of three different software applications: LIWC, WordSmith and ALIAS WISER.

In order to gain a deeper understanding of the specific categories which best discriminate between both sublanguages, two classification methods have been used, namely binary logistic regression and discriminant function analysis (DFA, hereafter), depending on how well the underlying data met their statistical requirements. The latter makes more demanding requirements on the data, since it assumes that the dependent variable is categorical –which happens to be the case in the present study– and shares all the usual assumptions of correlation, requiring linear and homoscedastic relationships –homogeneity of variances– and normal distribution of the interval or continuous data (Cantos, 2013). Nonetheless, DFA is known to be robust even when these assumptions are violated, as stated in most modern textbooks about multivariate statistics (e.g., Tabachnick & Fidell, 2013). As far as the subcorpora are concerned, a one-sample Kolmogorov-Smirnov test provided evidence against the null hypothesis, implying that the samples had not been drawn from a normal population. The distributions of the variables were found to be significant, thus a binary logistic regression was conducted instead.

As regards the calculations involved, DFA is broken down into a two-step process: first, a test is used to check whether the discriminant model as a whole is significant. In this case, Wilks' Lambda ($\lambda$) has been applied as a multi-variable measure of group means. Providing that the test reveals significance, the individual independent variables are then assessed to check which differ significantly in mean by group and these are used to classify the dependent variable. As a result, this test enabled the evaluation of the categories at a global level. This statistical analysis predicts a categorical dependent variable, the grouping variable –in this case, likelihood of veracity or deception– by one or more continuous or binary independent variables, namely the predictor variables. DFA is useful in determining whether a set of variables is effective in predicting category membership, since it assigns individuals, for whom several variables have been measured, to certain groups already identified in the sample (Almela ct al., 2022; Cantos, 2013). It answers the question of whether a combination of variables can be used to predict group membership. Thus, it determines the variables which discriminate between two or more naturally occurring groups, that is to say, truthful and untruthful accounts in the present study. The main difference with cluster analysis is that DFA is used for verifying that apparent clusters are real and for deciding to which cluster a new individual should be assigned.

From the set of independent variables used for separating cases, DFA creates new variables based on linear combinations which separate the groups as far apart as possible. The performance of the model is usually reported in terms of classification accuracy, with a percentage figure indicating how many cases would be correctly assigned to their groups using the new variables from DFA. The new variables can also be used to classify a new set of cases. It is worth noting that this analysis performs a previous significance test which checks whether the discriminant model as a whole is significant. If this is the case, then the individual independent variables are assessed to see which differ significantly in mean by group and these are used to classify the dependent variable.

Like DFA, logistic regression is a technique in which a set of predictors is used to determine group membership, but, as mentioned above, does not impose restrictive normality assumptions on the predictors. Even though DFA is known to be robust even when these assumptions are violated, as noted above, logistic regression was applied to the analysis of the individual subcorpora, as only a few variables met the requirements of normality and only 200 cases were involved. Two methods of binary logistic regression have been used for the sake of a double-check process: a backward stepwise method and a forward stepwise method. The former appears to be the preferred method in exploratory analyses (Hosmer and Lemeshow, 2000); it begins with a saturated model, and variables are eliminated from the model in an iterative process. The fit of the model is tested after the elimination of each variable to ensure that the model still adequately fits the data, and the analysis is completed when no more variables can be eliminated from the model. This type of regression calculates the probability of success over failure, and the results are in the form of an odds ratio. A Wald test has been used to assess the statistical significance of each coefficient ($\beta$) in the model, obtaining a Wald statistic with a chi-square distribution. This has enabled the preliminary selection of predictors. However, authors like Menard (1995) and Cohen et al. (2002) have identified problems with the use of the Wald statistic, mainly related to large or extremely low coefficients; they often tend to have associated inflated standard errors, which increases the probability of a Type-II error. Table 3.5 shows in green an instance of the variables with very high odd ratios and standard errors higher than 1, the results corresponding to the topic of good friend in English.

| | B | E.T. | Wald | d.f. | Sig. | Exp(B) | C.I. 95.0% for exp(B) | |
|---|---|---|---|---|---|---|---|---|
| | | | | | | | Lower | Upper |
| Sixltr | -.567 | .166 | 11.657 | 1 | .001 | .567 | .410 | .785 |
| Dash | -.977 | .278 | 12.365 | 1 | .000 | .377 | .219 | .649 |
| Parenth | -39.428 | 18551.472 | .000 | 1 | .998 | .000 | .000 | . |
| I | -.245 | .101 | 5.932 | 1 | .015 | .782 | .642 | .953 |
| You | .680 | .239 | 8.073 | 1 | .004 | 1.974 | 1.235 | 3.155 |
| Other | .852 | .160 | 28.473 | 1 | .000 | 2.345 | 1.715 | 3.208 |
| Negate | .659 | .212 | 9.635 | 1 | .002 | 1.933 | 1.275 | 2.930 |
| Preps | .214 | .092 | 5.355 | 1 | .021 | 1.238 | 1.033 | 1.484 |
| Posfeel | .819 | .273 | 9.005 | 1 | .003 | 2.268 | 1.329 | 3.873 |
| Optim | -.746 | .251 | 8.797 | 1 | .003 | .474 | .290 | .777 |
| Discrep | -.291 | .145 | 4.036 | 1 | .045 | .747 | .563 | .993 |
| Friends | -1.062 | .281 | 14.241 | 1 | .000 | .346 | .199 | .600 |
| Family | -1.616 | .446 | 13.113 | 1 | .000 | .199 | .083 | .477 |
| Humans | .733 | .253 | 8.376 | 1 | .004 | 2.082 | 1.267 | 3.421 |
| School | .630 | .202 | 9.675 | 1 | .002 | 1.877 | 1.262 | 2.791 |
| Achieve | .665 | .210 | 9.994 | 1 | .002 | 1.944 | 1.288 | 2.937 |
| Money | 1.214 | .418 | 8.444 | 1 | .004 | 3.366 | 1.485 | 7.633 |
| Sexual | -1.250 | .510 | 6.005 | 1 | .014 | .286 | .105 | .779 |
| Mean_word_length | 13.213 | 3.217 | 16.868 | 1 | .000 | 547552.1 | 999.872 | 3E+008 |
| Sentences | 55.691 | 16.238 | 11.762 | 1 | .001 | 2E+024 | 2E+010 | 1E+038 |
| One_letterW | 42.906 | 13.802 | 9.664 | 1 | .002 | 4E+018 | 7681314 | 2E+030 |

65

| | | | | | | | | |
|---|---|---|---|---|---|---|---|---|
| Two_letterW | 23.391 | 8.236 | 8.067 | 1 | .005 | 1E+010 | 1407.368 | 1E+017 |
| Seven_letterW | 26.494 | 14.314 | 3.426 | 1 | .064 | 3E+011 | .210 | 5E+023 |

Table 3.5 Example of the variables in the equation using a backward stepwise method

On the other hand, forward stepwise methods start with a model which does not include any of the predictors. Gradually, among the variables with a significance value lower than 0.05, the one with the largest score is selected and added to the model. In this case, a likelihood ratio method has been adopted, since, as Hosmer and Lemeshow (2000) explain it, the change in a -2 log-likelihood is generally more reliable than the Wald statistic. This guarantees that the variables chosen by both methods provide a good model; see Table 3.6 for the predictors finally included in the model after applying both methods. The easiest value to interpret is Exp(B), which represents the ratio change in the odds of the event of interest for a one-unit change in the predictor (Cohen et al., 2002).

|  | B | S.E. | Wald | df | Sig. | Exp(B) |
|---|---|---|---|---|---|---|
| Step 9   Dash | -.284 | .147 | 3.743 | 1 | .053 | .753 |
| I | -.152 | .052 | 8.637 | 1 | .003 | .859 |
| Other | .333 | .065 | 26.485 | 1 | .000 | 1.395 |
| Friends | -.539 | .139 | 15.130 | 1 | .000 | .583 |
| Family | -.843 | .274 | 9.498 | 1 | .002 | .430 |
| Humans | .453 | .165 | 7.560 | 1 | .006 | 1.573 |
| Money | .492 | .259 | 3.616 | 1 | .057 | 1.636 |
| Sexual | -.644 | .300 | 4.626 | 1 | .031 | .525 |

Table 3.6 Example of the variables in the equation using a forward stepwise method

In order to obtain more reliable classification results, a random sample of cases has been automatically generated for each topic to create a logistic regression model, setting the remaining contributions aside to validate the analysis. The reason for using a validation set is that classifications based upon the cases used to create the model tend to yield an inflated rate; thus, subset validation tends to be more reliable (Effron et al., 2004). It is worth noting that a Bernoulli distribution has been used to randomly generate the values of the variable *validate* with a probability parameter of 0.70, this variable taking values of 0 and 1. That is to say, approximately 70 percent of the truthful and untruthful statements will have a validate value of 1, being used to create the model, whereas the remaining statements will be used to validate the model results.

In sum, the present chapter has addressed two main areas, namely the research questions which have been raised and the method which is followed in order to conduct the study. The type of research on which the study is based responds to a quasi-experimental design, and the results will be provided and discussed in Chapter 4 and Chapter 5.

# CHAPTER 4. Study 1: Low-stakes deception

## 4.1 Introduction

The present chapter deals with the analysis of Study 1. These results are presented, analyzed and evaluated in order to answer the following research questions:

(1) How successful are LIWC categories and the further stylometric dimensions in low-stakes deception classification in English and in Spanish?

(2) Are there any linguistic cues to deception specific to certain topics?

Specifically, the main aim of this research is to explore the linguistic cues to low-stakes deception in written language both in English and Spanish, performing a contrastive analysis between both languages. Finally, the main limitations of the analysis are exposed.

## 4.2 Linguistic analysis

Variables are the operationalized way in which the attributes of objects are represented for further data processing (Babbie, 2009). Values of each variable are statistically distributed across the domain, which is the set of all possible values that a variable is allowed to have. The values must be defined for each variable, since domains can range from dichotomous or binary variables to multi-way variables, with a higher level of measurement.

In this case, a set of variables has been taken in view of the previous research on deception detection, commented on in Chapter 2. Specifically, the categories within the four broad LIWC dimensions have been considered, in addition to some further stylometric variables comprised within the stylistic profiling of the corpus.

### 4.2.1 LIWC variables

First of all, most of the basic psychologically meaningful categories contained in LIWC (Pennebaker et al., 2001) and described in Chapter 2 have been used. Certain selected categories are not included in the software application by default, namely period, comma, colon, semicolon, exclamation, dash, quote, apostrophe, parenthesis, and other punctuation. It is also worth noting that all the variables selected from LIWC reflect the percentage of total words, with three exceptions: raw word count, words per sentence, and percentage of interrogative sentences.

As explained in Chapter 2, the LIWC dictionary generally arranges categories hierarchically. Thus, some of the categories are the sum of others. For example, the category "Total pronouns" comprises "1st person singular", "1st person plural", "Total 1st person", "Total 2nd person", and "Total 3rd person". The categories "1st person singular" and "1st person plural", in turn, are both subsumed under "Total 1st person". Some previous studies such as

Newman et al. (2003) and Fornaciari and Poesio (2011) explore categories from different levels in the hierarchy using the same experiment. In ML classification and statistical techniques, this can result in redundancy, which may yield misleading results. As suggested by Picornell (2013) and Almela (2021a), in this case results might be skewed by counting those variables twice. In order to avoid this, there are two options: either removing the hierarchically superior categories, or keeping them and leaving the inferior categories out. In this case, the first option has been selected so as to keep the most specific information. Table 4.1 shows the LIWC categories removed and their correspondences. The first column contains the highest categories, the second one the subcategories, and the third one the subcategories of the previous subcategories –it is worth noticing that the categories which involve no complexity are not contained in this table. Categories in red are the most general ones, which have been altogether removed. These categories may comprise either categories in purple, which in turn comprise other lower categories, or just green ones, which are the terminal part of the sequence. Only the latter have been kept.

| I. Linguistic dimensions | | | |
|---|---|---|---|
| Total pronouns | Total 1$^{st}$ person | 1$^{st}$ person singular | |
| | | 1$^{st}$ person plural | |
| | Total 2$^{nd}$ person | - | |
| | Total 3$^{rd}$ person | - | |
| **II. Psychological processes** | | | |
| Affective or emotional processes | Positive emotions | Positive feelings | |
| | | Optimism and energy | |
| | Negative emotions | Anxiety or fear | |
| | | Anger | |
| | | Sadness or depression | |
| Cognitive processes | Causation | - | |
| | Insight | - | |
| | Discrepancy | - | |
| | Inhibition | - | |
| | Tentative | - | |
| | Certainty | - | |
| Sensory and perceptual processes | Seeing | - | |
| | Hearing | - | |
| | Feeling | - | |
| Social processes | Communication | - | |
| | Other references to people | 1$^{st}$ person plural | |
| | | Total 2$^{nd}$ person | |
| | | Total 3$^{rd}$ person | |
| | Friends | - | |
| | Family | - | |
| | Humans | - | |
| **III. Relativity** | | | |
| Time | Past tense verb | - | |
| | Present tense verb | - | |
| | Future tense verb | - | |
| Space | Up | - | |
| | Down | - | |
| | Inclusive | - | |
| | Exclusive | - | |
| **IV. Personal concerns** | | | |
| Occupation | School | - | |
| | Job or work | - | |
| | Achievement | - | |
| Leisure activity | Home | - | |
| | Sports | - | |
| | Television and movies | - | |
| | Music | - | |
| Metaphysical issues | Money and financial issues | - | |
| | Religion | - | |
| | Death and dying | - | |

| Physical states and functions | Body states, symptoms | - |
| | Sex and sexuality | - |
| | Eating, drinking, dieting | - |
| | Sleeping, dreaming | - |
| | Grooming | - |
| | Swearing | - |

Table 4.1 Selection of LIWC categories for the experiment

### 4.2.2 Further stylometric variables

There are some linguistic features not included in LIWC standard linguistic dimensions, which has been deemed relevant for the present study. As regards their computation, they have been obtained by means of the statistics worked out by Wordsmith Tools 8.0[9].

The first of these variables is standardized type/token ratio; as commented on above, the non-standardized version of this ratio was included in LIWC standard linguistic dimensions, but it has been proved to be too size-dependent as an index of lexical richness (Chipere et al., 2004). Thus, the discriminatory power of the original version of the ratio may be greater due to the disparities among the values for the different texts. However, it is not as reliable a measure as the standardized version. On the other hand, word length has also been considered. Despite the fact that a category similar to "complex words" was already included in LIWC, namely "Sixltr", all words longer than 6 letters were comprised. Since the general agreement in corpus linguistics is that complex words should include any word consisting of 8 or more letters (Cantos and

---

[9] Commercially available at www.lexically.net/wordsmith/

Almela, 2019), their frequency has been used for the calculation of one of the independent variables: the ratio of complex words to the number of tokens. Similarly, the ratios of the total amount of 1, 2, 3, 4, 5, 6, and 7-letter words to the number of tokens have been worked out. In addition to this, average word length (in characters) and average text length (in sentences) have also been considered in this section (see Scott, 2020a; 2020b).

## 4.3 Results and discussion

This section addresses the results yielded by the application of the statistical classification techniques implemented. As explained in the previous chapter, the statistical classification techniques implemented help gain a deeper understanding of the specific categories which best discriminate between both sublanguages. First, the results are presented for English and Spanish. Then, the results from the analysis of the individual subcorpora are evaluated.

### 4.3.1 Results for English

First of all, as shown in Table 4.5, Wilks' lambda confirms that the variables in combination successfully discriminate between truthful and untruthful statements (Wilks' $\lambda = 0.756$, $\chi^2 = 166.3$, $p = 0.000$). Smaller values of Wilks' lambda indicate greater discriminatory ability of the function. In addition, the associated chi-square statistic tests the hypothesis that the means of the functions listed are equal across groups. Table 4.2 displays the results of a one-way ANOVA for the independent variable using the grouping variable as the factor, and, if the significance value is lower than 0.10, the variable remarkably contributes to the model. Thus, according to the results, every variable in Table 4.3 is significant. Ranking the F-ratios –equality of group means– identifies word count as the best single predictor. Figure 4.1 reflects the importance of other predictors from a distance of 8 points, namely insight, $3^{rd}$ person, friends, $1^{st}$ person singular, exclusive words, $2^{nd}$ person, inclusive words, and discrepancy.

| Test of function(s) | Wilks' lambda | Chi-square | df | Sig. |
|:---:|:---:|:---:|:---:|:---:|
| 1 | .756 | 166.341 | 9 | .000 |

Table 4.2 Wilks' lambda for English

| Predictors | F | Sig. |
|:---:|:---:|:---:|
| WC | 44.473 | .000 |
| Insight | 36.562 | .000 |
| Other | 35.865 | .000 |
| Friends | 32.265 | .000 |
| I | 31.928 | .000 |
| Excl | 28.640 | .000 |
| You | 25.481 | .000 |
| Incl | 22.985 | .000 |
| Discrep | 21.206 | .000 |

Table 4.3 F-ratios for English

75

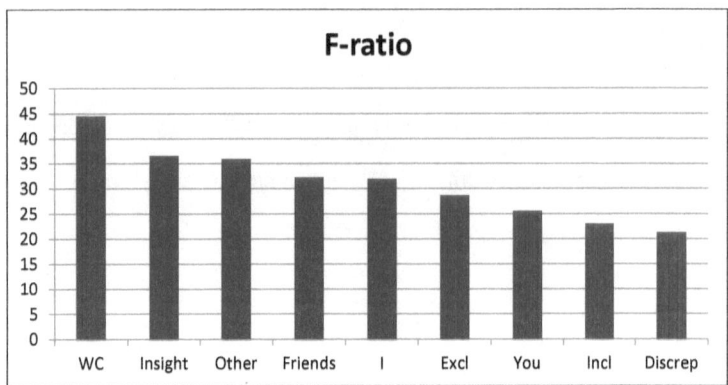

Figure 4.1 F-ratios for English graph

These results give relevant information concerning the most important predictors for the English corpus. Nonetheless, this information would be incomplete without the Fisher linear discriminant functions (see Table 4.4), which broaden knowledge on the variables substantially contributing to the ascription of statements to the group of truthful or untruthful texts in the model. Specifically, the discriminant model assigns the case to the group whose classification function obtained the highest score. In this respect, the categories that contribute the most to deception detection are 2nd and 3rd person. On the contrary, a strong presence of word count –that is to say, longer statements–, 1st person singular, words related to insight, discrepancy, friends, and inclusive and exclusive words are fairly characteristic of truthful texts.

76

|            | Deception | |
|------------|-----------|----------|
|            | No        | Yes      |
| WC         | .074      | .057     |
| I          | .096      | .005     |
| You        | .193      | .321     |
| Other      | .082      | .276     |
| Insight    | .829      | .605     |
| Discrep    | .798      | .701     |
| Friends    | .717      | .335     |
| Incl       | .915      | .830     |
| Excl       | .816      | .678     |
| (Constant) | -11.443   | -8.608   |

Table 4.4 Fisher linear discriminant functions for English

This DFA model successfully classified 72.3% of the original grouped cases (see Table 4.5), and cross-validation was similarly successful, with the leave-one-out classification method seeing 70.8% of the statements correctly classified. It is worth noting that the percentage of truthful and untruthful statements correctly classified in the cross-validation was remarkably similar (70.7% vs 71.0%). This means in practice that 212 truthful and 213 untruthful texts were classified as such.

| | Deception | | Predicted group membership | | Total |
|---|---|---|---|---|---|
| | | | No | Yes | 1 |
| Original(a) | Count | No | 219 | 81 | 300 |
| | | Yes | 85 | 215 | 300 |
| | % | No | 73.0 | 27.0 | 100.0 |
| | | Yes | 28.3 | 71.7 | 100.0 |
| Cross-validated (b) | Count | No | 212 | 88 | 300 |
| | | Yes | 87 | 213 | 300 |
| | % | No | 70.7 | 29.3 | 100.0 |
| | | Yes | 29.0 | 71.0 | 100.0 |
| (a) 72.3% of original grouped cases correctly classified. | | | | | |
| (b) 70.8% of cross-validated grouped cases correctly classified. | | | | | |

Table 4.5 Classification results from DFA for English

### 4.3.2 Results for Spanish

Much like the English corpus, a DFA has been applied to the Spanish corpus. Table 4.6 shows a successful discrimination between both kinds of statements (Wilks' $\lambda = 0.699$, $\chi^2 = 210.7$, p = 0.000).

78

| Test of function(s) | Wilks' lambda | Chi-square | df | Sig. |
|---|---|---|---|---|
| 1 | .699 | 210.704 | 17 | .000 |

Table 4.6 Wilks' lambda for Spanish

Again, text length proves to be the best single predictor, as shown in Table 4.7 and Figure 4.2. Curiously enough, in this case the difference between this predictor and the next one in importance is 20 points, which is more than twice the difference observed in the English corpus. Despite this fact, the F-ratio for the next predictor, 1st person singular, is still rather high. There are some other variables identified as predictors shared with the English corpus, namely 2nd person, friends, insight, exclusive words, and 3rd person. The remaining predictors for the Spanish corpus are words related to certainty, humans, sexual, number, anger, semicolon, past, assent, future, and tentative words. Figure 4.3 shows the distribution of the predictor categories in both corpora.

| Predictors | F | Sig. |
|:---:|:---:|:---:|
| WC | 69.812 | .000 |
| I | 49.259 | .000 |
| Certain | 39.199 | .000 |
| You | 33.516 | .000 |
| Friends | 30.167 | .000 |
| Humans | 27.682 | .000 |
| Insight | 25.708 | .000 |
| Excl | 23.601 | .000 |
| Sexual | 21.871 | .000 |
| Number | 20.568 | .000 |
| Anger | 19.397 | .000 |
| SemiC | 18.329 | .000 |
| Other | 17.495 | .000 |
| Past | 16.643 | .000 |
| Assent | 15.909 | .000 |
| Future | 15.239 | .000 |
| Tentat | 14.709 | .000 |

Table 4.7 F-ratios for Spanish

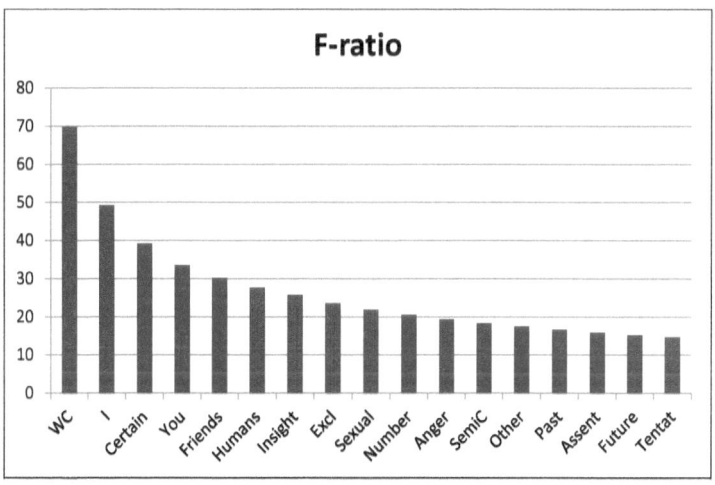

Figure 4.2 F-ratios for Spanish graph

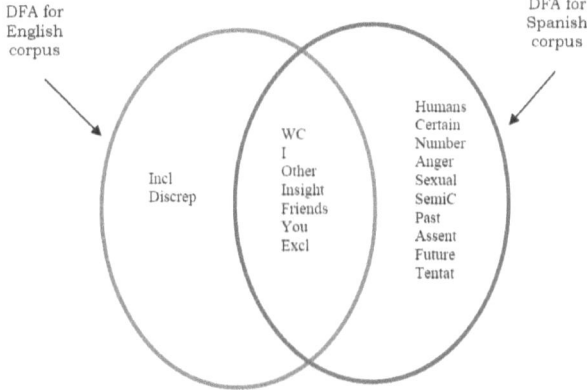

Figure 4.3 Venn diagram of the predictor categories identified by the DFA in the

English and Spanish corpora

On the other hand, the Fisher linear discriminant functions show that the categories that contribute the most to the model concerning untruthfulness are $2^{nd}$ and $3^{rd}$ person –predictors shared by both corpora–, certainty, humans, and future, whereas a strong presence of exceptional text length, semicolon, $1^{st}$ person singular, words indicating assent, number, anxiety, insight, tentative, friends, past, sexuality, and exclusive words typically characterizes truthful statements in Spanish (see Table 4.8).

In this case, the DFA model is slightly more successful than with the English corpus: 76.3% of the original grouped cases were correctly classified (see Table 4.9), and the leave-one-out classification method has achieved a success rate of 74.0%. As regards the percentage of truthful and untruthful statements correctly classified in the cross-validation, the former is slightly more successful than the latter (75.7% vs 72.3%). Specifically, there is a difference of ten more statements correctly classified.

|  | Deception | |
|---|---|---|
|  | No | Yes |
| WC | .096 | .077 |
| SemiC | .675 | -.055 |
| I | .435 | .222 |
| You | .169 | .397 |
| Other | .842 | .907 |
| Assent | -.439 | -.156 |
| Number | .459 | .279 |
| Anx | 1.350 | 1.051 |
| Insight | .901 | .712 |
| Tentat | .682 | .557 |
| Certain | -.007 | .194 |
| Friends | .642 | .361 |
| Humans | .549 | .736 |
| Past | .607 | .485 |
| Future | -.261 | .029 |
| Excl | .837 | .615 |
| Sexual | .657 | .400 |
| (Constant) | -13.647 | -11.167 |

Table 4.8 Fisher linear discriminant functions for Spanish

| | | | Predicted group membership | | Total |
|---|---|---|---|---|---|
| | | Deception | No | Yes | 1 |
| | | | No | 233 | 67 | 300 |
| Original (a) | Count | No | 233 | 67 | 300 |
| | | Yes | 75 | 225 | 300 |
| | % | No | 77.7 | 22.3 | 100.0 |
| | | Yes | 25.0 | 75.0 | 100.0 |
| Cross-validated (b) | Count | No | 227 | 73 | 300 |
| | | Yes | 83 | 217 | 300 |
| | % | No | 75.7 | 24.3 | 100.0 |
| | | Yes | 27.7 | 72.3 | 100.0 |
| (a) 76.3% of original grouped cases correctly classified. | | | | | |
| (b) 74.0% of cross-validated grouped cases correctly classified. | | | | | |

Table 4.9 Classification results from DFA for Spanish

### 4.3.3 Subcorpora in English

As commented on in the previous chapter, a one-sample Kolmogorov-Smirnov test provided evidence against the null hypothesis for the three subcorpora in English, implying that the samples had not been drawn from a normal population. The distributions of the variables were found to be significant, thus binary logistic regressions were conducted instead of DFA.

From the two methods of binary logistic regression used, the backward stepwise method begins with a saturated model, and variables are eliminated from the model in an iterative process. The fit of the model is tested after the elimination of each variable to ensure that the model still adequately fits the data, and the analysis is completed when no more variables can be eliminated from the model. The variables kept in the last step are WC, Sixltr, Comma, Dash, Quote, Apostro, We, Other, Number, Anger, Sad, Cause, Insight, Incl, Money, Death, and Sexual.

A Wald test has been used to assess the statistical significance of each coefficient (β) in the model, so as to make the preliminary selection of predictors. Following Cohen et al. (2002) and Menard (1995), large and extremely low coefficients with associated inflated standard errors must be discarded, since they increase the probability of a Type-II error; this usually includes variables with standard errors higher than 1. Subsequently, a forward stepwise binary logistic regression has been performed on the preselected variables. In terms of significance, this procedure reports the Hosmer-Lemeshow goodness-of-fit statistics, which is useful to determine whether the built model reasonably approximates the behavior of the data. It indicates a poor fit if the significance value is less than 0.05. Here, the model adequately fits the data (p = .899).

Following Hosmer and Lemeshow (2000), if there is a statistically significant relationship, the pattern of significance in the individual Wald statistics is potentially useful to interpret the role of the variable in predicting membership in dependent variable categories. However, the authors identify the likelihood ratio method as more effective in identifying relationships than the Wald statistics for the individual logistic regression equations. That is to say, the change in a -2 log-likelihood is generally more reliable than the Wald statistic.

Table 4.10 shows the predictors finally included in the model after applying both methods with their corresponding coefficients. The easiest value to interpret is Exp(B), which represents the ratio change in the odds of the event of interest for a one-unit change in the predictor (Cohen et al., 2002). As in the previous test, large and extremely low coefficients with associated inflated standard errors must be discarded, since they increase the probability of a Type-II error (Cohen et al., 2002; Menard, 1995). However, the coefficients and the standard errors of all the predictors kept in the last step prove to be adequate. As regards the coefficient ($\beta$) of logistic regression, it is worth noting that it does not have the same straightforward interpretation as it does with linear regression (Efron et al., 2004), but its sign gives information on the truth value of the statements in the classification experiment. Specifically, positive values are indicative of predictors of untruthful statements, namely 1st person plural, 3rd person, causal words, and words related to sex, whereas negative values here are associated with truthful statements, in this case text length, words related to anger, sadness, insight, and inclusive words.

|         |        | B      | S.E. | Wald   | df | Sig. | Exp(B) |
|---------|--------|--------|------|--------|----|------|--------|
|         | WC     | -.047  | .011 | 19.664 | 1  | .000 | .954   |
|         | We     | .854   | .302 | 7.983  | 1  | .005 | 2.350  |
| Step 9  | Other  | .334   | .124 | 7.282  | 1  | .007 | 1.396  |
|         | Anger  | -.627  | .212 | 8.777  | 1  | .003 | .534   |
|         | Sad    | -1.205 | .483 | 6.221  | 1  | .013 | .300   |
|         | Cause  | .742   | .268 | 7.670  | 1  | .006 | 2.100  |
|         | Insight| -1.064 | .219 | 23.615 | 1  | .000 | .345   |
|         | Incl   | -.284  | .111 | 6.594  | 1  | .010 | .752   |
|         | Sexual | .289   | .130 | 4.947  | 1  | .026 | 1.335  |

Table 4.10 Variables in the last step of the equation in the forward stepwise logistic

regression for the abortion topic

Once a reliable set of predictors has been selected, the classification
results are to be explored. As explained above, a random sample of cases has
been automatically generated for each topic to create a logistic regression
model, setting the remaining contributions aside to validate the analysis and
obtain a more reliable classification rate. By means of random generation and
of a Bernoulli distribution, approximately 70% of the truthful and untruthful
statements have been used to create the model, whereas the remaining
statements have been used to validate the model results. As can be seen in
Table 4.11, the model is successful in the classification of the original cases

87

(69.6%), although it is remarkably more successful in the validation subset, its rate being 75.4%, with 75.8% of truthful statements correctly classified and 75% of untruthful statements classified as such –there is just one less statement correctly classified.

| Observed | | | Predicted | | | | | |
|---|---|---|---|---|---|---|---|---|
| | | | Selected cases | | | Unselected cases | | |
| | | | Deception | | | Deception | | |
| | | | | | Percent. | | | Percent. |
| | | | No | Yes | Correct | No | Yes | Correct |
| Step 9 | Deception | No | 48 | 19 | 71.6 | 25 | 8 | 75.8 |
| | | Yes | 22 | 46 | 67.6 | 8 | 24 | 75.0 |
| | Overall Percentage | | | | 69.6 | | | 75.4 |

Table 4.11 Classification results in the forward stepwise logistic regression for the

abortion topic

As can be seen above, the model obtained includes several unique predictors. Concerning the linguistic dimension, 1st person plural has been identified as a predictor of untruthfulness. Despite having been usually studied as a subcategory of the total 1st person (e.g. Newman et al., 2003), from a psycholinguistic perspective it falls within the category of references to others (Pennebaker et al., 2001). Thus, it indicates detachment from the self, like the 2nd and 3rd person or humans, commented on in previous sections. As regards psychological processes, two negative emotions have also proved significant for this model: anger and sadness. This finding is in line with the discriminant function of anxiety in the whole Spanish corpus, thus the same explanation applies in this case. Although the experiment deals with low-consequence deception, abortion is a topic about which participants may feel guilty. In line with Ali and Levine (2008), it may be that the identification of speakers with their real opinions on so controversial a topic leads to higher levels of anger and sadness, successfully discriminating truthful statements. Last but not least, a cognitive process worth mentioning in this model is causation. As has been seen, the remaining cognitive processes involved in the global discriminant models had proved significant for truth, especially those involving cognitive verbs. However, in this case the category causation is a good predictor of untruthfulness, in line with Hartwig et al. (2006) and Vrij et al. (2008). This apparent contradiction confirms the idea that exploring cognitive processes separately is more useful than taking them as a whole category.

As regards the prediction of membership in the death penalty subcorpus in English, the amount of valid variables preselected by the backward stepwise method is slightly larger than in the previous topic (see Table 4.12). In order to reduce the probability of a Type-II error, the large and extremely low coefficients with associated inflated standard errors have been discarded.

The subsequent forward stepwise binary logistic regression has been performed on the preselected variables. The Hosmer-Lemeshow goodness-of-fit statistics indicate that the model adequately fits the data (p = .519), that is to say, the built model reasonably approximates the behavior of the data. As far as the change in the -2 log-likelihood is concerned, in the death penalty subcorpus it has proved significant with three predictors: $1^{st}$ person singular, past and exclusive words. With these predictors, the model has been able to successfully classify 71.6% of truthful statements and 75% of untruthful ones of the original cases, with a global success rate of 73.3%, as shown in Table 4.13. With the validation subset, the model classifies 66.2% of correct cases. Most interestingly, the success rate in the case of the untruthful statements is significantly higher than with the truthful ones (78.1% vs 54.4%). It is worth noting that this subcorpus, the death penalty, has registered the lowest success rate in English.

As can be seen, this model does not include any unique predictors, but three cues discriminating truth which are common to either both languages –$1^{st}$ person singular and exclusive words– or to the Spanish corpus –past tense. It is worth noting that there is no predictor for untruthfulness. On the contrary, most predictors in the good friend subcorpus in English are significant for untruthfulness, two of them being unique: money and financial issues, and family. A plausible explanation for the weight of the former category as to the subject of good friend is the metaphorical usage of words such as *costar (to cost), deuda (debt), fortuna (fortune),* and *ganancia (profit),* derived from the metaphor FRIENDSHIP IS A VALUABLE COMMODITY, studied by Kövecses (2000). According to Gibbs (1994), metaphorical language is frequently used to avoid responsibility for the significance of what is communicated, and this may be the reason why it is significant for untruthful accounts on friendship. The other unique predictor in this model, family, belongs to social processes, and is relevant to the classification of truthful statements. The usual identification of real friends with relatives seems fairly frequent, hence the significance of the category in this subcorpus.

| | B | S.E. | Wald | df | Sig. | Exp(B) |
|---|---|---|---|---|---|---|
| WC | -.025 | .010 | 6.342 | 1 | .012 | .976 |
| WPS | .115 | .050 | 5.242 | 1 | .022 | 1.122 |
| Sixltr | -.440 | .239 | 3.384 | 1 | .066 | .644 |
| Period | -1.085 | .374 | 8.410 | 1 | .004 | .338 |
| Dash | -.932 | .474 | 3.871 | 1 | .049 | .394 |
| Apostro | .776 | .343 | 5.106 | 1 | .024 | 2.173 |
| OtherP | -1.191 | .563 | 4.486 | 1 | .034 | .304 |
| I | -1.374 | .271 | 25.735 | 1 | .000 | .253 |
| Negate | -.347 | .148 | 5.495 | 1 | .019 | .706 |
| Posfeel | 1.097 | .489 | 5.035 | 1 | .025 | 2.995 |
| Tentat | -.423 | .143 | 8.773 | 1 | .003 | .655 |
| Certain | .364 | .215 | 2.857 | 1 | .091 | 1.439 |
| Feel | .866 | .404 | 4.589 | 1 | .032 | 2.378 |
| Past | -.635 | .186 | 11.638 | 1 | .001 | .530 |
| Present | .190 | .088 | 4.649 | 1 | .031 | 1.209 |
| Future | .439 | .166 | 6.987 | 1 | .008 | 1.551 |
| Excl | -.315 | .111 | 8.064 | 1 | .005 | .730 |

| | | | | | | |
|---|---|---|---|---|---|---|
| Job | -.865 | .319 | 7.343 | 1 | .007 | .421 |
| Body | -.847 | .295 | 8.213 | 1 | .004 | .429 |
| STTR | -.322 | .131 | 6.069 | 1 | .014 | .725 |

Table 4.12 Variables in the last step of the equation in the backward stepwise logistic regression for the death penalty topic

| | | | Predicted | | | | | |
|---|---|---|---|---|---|---|---|---|
| | | | Selected cases | | | Unselected cases | | |
| | | | Deception | | Percent. | Deception | | Percent. |
| | Observed | | No | Yes | Correct | No | Yes | Correct |
| Step 3 | Deception | No | 48 | 19 | 71.6 | 18 | 15 | 54.5 |
| | | Yes | 17 | 51 | 75.0 | 7 | 25 | 78.1 |
| | Overall Percentage | | | | 73.3 | | | 66.2 |

Table 4.13 Classification results in the forward stepwise logistic regression for the death penalty topic

In line with the abortion topic, for the good friend subcorpus a total of 17 valid variables out of the set of 76 have been preselected by the backward stepwise method, leaving aside the discarded variables on the grounds of abnormal coefficients and standard errors: Sixltr, Dash, I, You, Other, Negate, Preps, Posfeel, Optim, Discrep, Friends, Family, Humans, School, Achieve, Money, and Sexual.

In this case, the model built by the forward stepwise logistic regression adequately fits the data (p = .194). This goodness-of-fit statistic describes a model comprising six significant predictors, namely 3rd person, words related to friendship and humans, 2nd person, and words concerning money and family. Like in the previous cases, their significance is assessed in terms of the changes in the -2 log-likelihood.

Table 4.14 shows the predictors finally included in the model after applying both methods with their corresponding coefficients. Positive values, indicative of predictors of untruthful statements, correspond to 2nd and 3rd person, as well as words related to humans and money. On the other hand, terms concerning friendship and family are associated here with truthful statements.

| | | B | S.E. | Wald | df | Sig. | Exp(B) |
|---|---|---|---|---|---|---|---|
| Step 6 | You | .387 | .139 | 7.769 | 1 | .005 | 1.472 |
| | Other | .325 | .071 | 20.983 | 1 | .000 | 1.384 |
| | Friends | -.509 | .161 | 10.040 | 1 | .002 | .601 |
| | Family | -.631 | .300 | 4.419 | 1 | .036 | .532 |
| | Humans | .584 | .191 | 9.378 | 1 | .002 | 1.793 |
| | Money | .558 | .268 | 4.344 | 1 | .037 | 1.747 |

Table 4.14 Variables in the last step of the equation in the forward stepwise logistic regression for the good friend topic in English

Regarding the success rate of this model, it is 77% with the original cases and 78.5% with the validation subset, which is the highest rate obtained for English. In the first case, the proportion of untruthful statements correctly classified is slightly higher than the proportion of truthful ones (77.9% vs 76.1%), whereas the situation with the validation subset is exactly the opposite (78.1% vs 78.8%), as shown in Table 4.15. These are the best success rates in English.

| | | | Predicted | | | | | |
|---|---|---|---|---|---|---|---|---|
| | | | Selected cases | | | Unselected cases | | |
| | | | Deception | | Percent. | Deception | | Percent. |
| | Observed | | No | Yes | Correct | No | Yes | Correct |
| Step 8 | Deception | No | 51 | 16 | 76.1 | 26 | 7 | 78.8 |
| | | Yes | 15 | 53 | 77.9 | 7 | 25 | 78.1 |
| | Overall Percentage | | | | 77.0 | | | 78.5 |

Table 4.15 Classification results in the forward stepwise logistic regression for the good friend topic in English

### 4.3.4 Subcorpora in Spanish

In line with the English subcorpora, the distributions of the variables in the Spanish subcorpora were found to be significant by means of a one-sample

Kolmogorov-Smirnov test, hence the performance of logistic regressions on the data over DFA.

First of all, the amount of valid variables preselected for the bullfighting subcorpora by the backward stepwise method is similar to the English subcorpora (see Table 4.28). Variables with abnormal coefficients were also discarded for this and the rest of the Spanish subcorpora.

In this case, Table 4.16 shows how the Hosmer-Lemeshow goodness-of-fit statistic proves that the model built by the forward stepwise regression adequately fits the data (p = .755); this model comprises just three predictors. Interestingly enough, the model is rather similar to that built on the death penalty subcorpus, since it also included just three significant variables. Two of them were common to both subcorpora, namely 1$^{st}$ person and exclusive words; the other is text length.

Finally, another parallel with the death penalty subcorpus is that it is the one with the lowest success rate in its language. Specifically, 75.8% of the truthful statements and 65.6% of the untruthful ones were correctly classified within the validation subset, with an overall percentage of 70.8. As can be seen in Table 4.17, so far as the original cases are concerned, the overall success rate is 78.5%, the classification success being notable both with truthful statements –76.1%– and with untruthful ones –80.9%.

|  | B | S.E. | Wald | df | Sig. | Exp(B) |
|---|---|---|---|---|---|---|
| WC | -.030 | .007 | 16.578 | 1 | .000 | .970 |
| Period | -.984 | .376 | 6.858 | 1 | .009 | .374 |
| QMark | -1.455 | .505 | 8.295 | 1 | .004 | .233 |
| I | -1.024 | .217 | 22.192 | 1 | .000 | .359 |
| We | .674 | .203 | 11.058 | 1 | .001 | 1.962 |
| Other | -.182 | .098 | 3.428 | 1 | .064 | .834 |
| Optim | -.486 | .244 | 3.961 | 1 | .047 | .615 |
| Tentat | -.452 | .137 | 10.929 | 1 | .001 | .636 |
| See | -.667 | .279 | 5.725 | 1 | .017 | .513 |
| Hear | .771 | .449 | 2.955 | 1 | .086 | 2.163 |
| Comm | -.444 | .248 | 3.196 | 1 | .074 | .641 |
| Excl | -.683 | .177 | 14.901 | 1 | .000 | .505 |
| Job | -.780 | .304 | 6.601 | 1 | .010 | .458 |
| Achieve | .513 | .255 | 4.063 | 1 | .044 | 1.671 |
| TV | 2.666 | .738 | 13.047 | 1 | .000 | 14.376 |
| Money | 1.022 | .446 | 5.257 | 1 | .022 | 2.779 |
| Eating | -1.001 | .271 | 13.663 | 1 | .000 | .368 |

Table 4.16 Variables in the last step of the equation in the backward stepwise logistic regression for the bullfighting topic

| | | | Predicted | | | | | |
|---|---|---|---|---|---|---|---|---|
| | | | Selected cases | | | Unselected cases | | |
| | | | Deception | | | Deception | | |
| | | | No | Yes | Percent. Correct | No | Yes | Percent. Correct |
| | Observed | | | | | | | |
| Step 3 | Deception | No | 51 | 16 | 76.1 | 25 | 8 | 75.8 |
| | | Yes | 13 | 55 | 80.9 | 11 | 21 | 65.6 |
| | Overall Percentage | | | | 78.5 | | | 70.8 |

Table 4.17 Classification results in the forward stepwise logistic regression for the

bullfighting topic

When it comes to the homosexual adoption subcorpus, as shown in Table 4.18, a total of 22 valid variables out of the set of 76 have been preselected by the backward stepwise method, leaving aside the discarded variables on the grounds of abnormal coefficients and standard errors, which is the largest number in all the subcorpora.

In the forward stepwise logistic regression, the goodness-of-fit statistic shows that the model fits the data (p = .100), although its significance is not as evident as in the other subcorpora.

|  | B | S.E. | Wald | df | Sig. | Exp(B) |
|---|---|---|---|---|---|---|
| WC | -.038 | .010 | 15.362 | 1 | .000 | .963 |
| Apostro | 1.138 | .352 | 10.453 | 1 | .001 | 3.122 |
| I | -.861 | .355 | 5.891 | 1 | .015 | .423 |
| You | .758 | .255 | 8.854 | 1 | .003 | 2.134 |
| Negate | .518 | .203 | 6.470 | 1 | .011 | 1.678 |
| Article | .347 | .133 | 6.831 | 1 | .009 | 1.415 |
| Posfeel | -.894 | .295 | 9.200 | 1 | .002 | .409 |
| Anx | 1.451 | .744 | 3.805 | 1 | .051 | 4.267 |
| Anger | -2.088 | .748 | 7.794 | 1 | .005 | .124 |
| Hear | 1.255 | .560 | 5.022 | 1 | .025 | 3.509 |
| Feel | -.575 | .226 | 6.459 | 1 | .011 | .563 |
| Family | .427 | .150 | 8.057 | 1 | .005 | 1.532 |
| Humans | .281 | .143 | 3.852 | 1 | .050 | 1.325 |
| Future | .591 | .338 | 3.051 | 1 | .081 | 1.806 |
| Incl | .739 | .213 | 11.991 | 1 | .001 | 2.094 |
| Excl | -1.102 | .329 | 11.230 | 1 | .001 | .332 |
| Motion | 1.303 | .618 | 4.445 | 1 | .035 | 3.680 |
| Home | -.833 | .449 | 3.439 | 1 | .064 | .435 |
| Sexual | -.642 | .233 | 7.560 | 1 | .006 | .526 |
| STTR | .231 | .067 | 11.841 | 1 | .001 | 1.260 |

Table 4.18 Variables in the last step of the equation in the backward stepwise logistic regression for the homosexual adoption topic

Six predictors have been identified as significant on the grounds of the changes in the -2 log-likelihood, namely 1st person singular, text length, positive feelings, inclusive words, and terms related to humans and motion. The first three are predictors of truthful statements, and the remainder of untruthful ones, although motion is only near to significant (p = .057).

With these predictors, the model has been able to successfully classify 73.1% of truthful statements and 75% of untruthful ones of the original cases, with an overall success rate of 74.1% (see Table 4.19). With the validation subset, the model classifies 75.4% of correct cases. Interestingly enough, the success rate in the case of the untruthful statements is significantly higher than with the truthful ones (81.3% vs 69.7%), which is a similar situation with the death penalty subcorpus.

| | | | Predicted | | | | | |
| --- | --- | --- | --- | --- | --- | --- | --- | --- |
| | | | Selected cases | | | Unselected cases | | |
| | | | Deception | | Percent. | Deception | | Percent. |
| | Observed | | No | Yes | Correct | No | Yes | Correct |
| Step 6 | Deception | No | 49 | 18 | 73.1 | 23 | 10 | 69.7 |
| | | Yes | 17 | 51 | 75.0 | 6 | 26 | 81.3 |
| | Overall Percentage | | | | 74.1 | | | 75.4 |

Table 4.19 Classification results in the forward stepwise logistic regression for the homosexual adoption topic

Thus, two unique cues have proved relevant in the homosexual adoption model: positive feelings and motion. The former, which happens to be a positive emotional process, has proved a predictor of truth. This finding is in line with the negative emotional processes previously discussed, which were also significant for the discrimination of truthful statements. Thus, an alternative reason to that proposed by Newman et al. (2003) is suggested here. As explained above, in their study they find that negative emotion words are positively correlated with deception, but no relation is found with positive emotion. They explain the former finding on the grounds of the subject matter involved in the experiment, which may produce guilt and a sense of unease. Nevertheless, the present results reveal that all the categories related to emotion are positively correlated with truth, thus it may be that the identification of speakers with their real opinions on so controversial topics and their commitment to certain ideals lead to higher levels not only of anxiety, anger or sadness, but of emotion in general. Regarding motion words, they have proved significant for the classification of untruthful statements in this model. This is certainly in line with Newman et al., who explain it as follows:

> Because liars' stories are by definition fabricated, some of their cognitive resources are taken up by the effort of creating a believable story. Motion verbs (e.g. *walk, go, carry*) provide simple, concrete descriptions and are more readily accessible than words that focus on evaluations and judgments (e.g. *think, believe*) (2003: 672).

For the last subcorpus, good friend topic, the preliminary selection of valid variables made by the backward stepwise regression is shown in Table 4.20. When it comes to the forward stepwise method, it can be stated that the model adequately fits the data (p = .905). In fact, this is the best value for the Hosmer-Lemeshow statistic not only for Spanish but for the whole set of subcorpora.

This model is the one comprising the highest amount of predictors (see Table 4.21). Specifically, on the grounds of the changes in the -2 log-likelihood, certainty is the category with the greatest discriminatory power; other relevant predictors are number, 2nd person, text length, 1st person singular, 3rd person, quotation punctuation, words related to achievement, friendship, sadness, and inhibition.

|  | B | S.E. | Wald | df | Sig. | Exp(B) |
|---|---|---|---|---|---|---|
| WC | -.040 | .010 | 15.513 | 1 | .000 | .961 |
| Period | -.381 | .145 | 6.911 | 1 | .009 | .683 |
| SemiC | -1.842 | .551 | 11.162 | 1 | .001 | .158 |
| Quote | -1.302 | .593 | 4.826 | 1 | .028 | .272 |
| I | -.454 | .133 | 11.686 | 1 | .001 | .635 |
| We | -.319 | .154 | 4.273 | 1 | .039 | .727 |
| You | .726 | .259 | 7.883 | 1 | .005 | 2.068 |
| Other | .288 | .096 | 9.020 | 1 | .003 | 1.334 |
| Number | -1.433 | .386 | 13.757 | 1 | .000 | .239 |
| Posfeel | .443 | .190 | 5.441 | 1 | .020 | 1.557 |
| Sad | -2.031 | .710 | 8.171 | 1 | .004 | .131 |
| Inhib | -1.605 | .899 | 3.187 | 1 | .074 | .201 |
| Certain | .663 | .184 | 13.050 | 1 | .000 | 1.941 |
| Friends | -.699 | .232 | 9.068 | 1 | .003 | .497 |
| Future | 1.245 | .501 | 6.164 | 1 | .013 | 3.471 |
| Achieve | .823 | .285 | 8.310 | 1 | .004 | 2.277 |
| STTR | .038 | .018 | 4.299 | 1 | .038 | 1.039 |

Table 4.20 Variables in the last step of the equation in the backward stepwise logistic regression for the good friend topic in Spanish

| Predictors | Change in the -2 log-likelihood |
|---|---|
| Certain | 20.318 |
| Number | 16.850 |
| You | 16.755 |
| WC | 12.775 |
| I | 11.551 |
| Other | 11.546 |
| Quote | 10.989 |
| Achieve | 10.080 |
| Friends | 10.037 |
| Sad | 5.304 |
| Inhib | 4.629 |

Table 4.21 Changes in the -2 log-likelihood for the good friend topic in Spanish

Furthermore, this is the first time that a variable is included in the model with a relevant change in the -2 log-likelihood which proves not significant in the last step of the equation in the forward stepwise regression: quotation punctuation. Apart from this, positive values, indicative of predictors of untruthful statements, correspond to 2$^{nd}$ and 3$^{rd}$ person, and words concerning certainty and achievement, whereas text length, 1$^{st}$ person singular, number, terms related to sadness, inhibition, and friendship are associated in this case with truthful statements.

This model has identified two unique predictors for truth and untruthfulness respectively: inhibition and achievement. According to the Oxford Dictionary[10], the former entails a cognitive process by means of which there is a restraint on the direct expression of an instinct, expressed by words such as *abstenerse (refrain), detener (halt)* and *desistir (desist)*. Although this specific process has not been explored as such in deception detection literature, this is in line with the findings discussed above on the discriminant power of cognitive processes. On the other hand, together with the other specific cues related to personal concerns, achievement has proved significant for the classification of untruthful statements. A close parallel may be drawn between achievement and motion, which proved successful in the classification of untruthful statements in the homosexual adoption model. Lakoff's EVENT STRUCTURE metaphor and its submetaphor PURPOSES ARE DESTINATIONS (as cited in Kövecses, 2000: 53) are at the basis of this parallel. Thus, the same explanation advanced above applies in this case: the fabrication of a believable story or of a fake opinion is more easily performed by means of concrete descriptions and expressions to the detriment of markers of cognitive complexity.

---

[10] Available at http://oxforddictionaries.com/

| | | | Predicted | | | | |
|---|---|---|---|---|---|---|---|
| | | | Selected cases | | | Unselected cases | |
| | | | Deception | | Percent. | Deception | | Percent. |
| | | | No | Yes | Correct | No | Yes | Correct |
| | Observed | | | | | | | |
| Step 7 | Deception | No | 58 | 9 | 86.6 | 29 | 4 | 87.9 |
| | | Yes | 6 | 62 | 91.2 | 6 | 26 | 81.3 |
| | Overall Percentage | | | | 88.9 | | | 84.6 |

Table 4.22 Classification results in the forward stepwise logistic regression for the

good friend topic in Spanish


Finally, the remarkable success rates in this subcorpus are worth noting,

since it is 88.9% with the original cases and 84.6% with the validation subset

(see Table 4.22). In the first case, the proportion of untruthful statements

correctly classified is slightly higher than the proportion of truthful ones (91.2%

vs 86.6%), whereas the situation with the validation subset is exactly the

opposite (81.3% vs 87.9%). These are the best success rates in both languages.

### 4.3.5 Summary of results in both languages

In order to present a comprehensive picture of the effectiveness of the statistical

classification methods employed, a summary of the success rates is provided in

Table 4.23 and a visual representation in Figure 4.4. The experiments

conducted on the good friend subcorpora, both in English and Spanish, yield the best results within the set of each respective language. This is especially so in Spanish, where there is a difference of more than 9 points with the previous subcorpus in terms of success, homosexual adoption (84.6% vs 75.4%). In English, the good friend subcorpus, despite being the best one in this language, differs notably from the homologous subcorpus in Spanish; specifically, it scores 78.5%.

| | Subcorpus | Overall percentage correct |
|---|---|---|
| English | Abortion | 75.4 |
| | Death penalty | 66.2 |
| | Good friend | 78.5 |
| | All | 70.8 |
| Spanish | Bullfighting | 70.8 |
| | Homosexual adoption | 75.4 |
| | Good friend | 84.6 |
| | All | 74 |

Table 4.23 Classification results for all corpora

On the other hand, the worst rate in English is obtained by the death penalty, where a difference of more than 9 points exists with the next subcorpus, abortion (66.2% vs 75.4%), with the worst score in Spanish corresponding to bullfighting (70.8%). As regards the global corpora, the classification method performs better with the Spanish corpus than with the English one (74% vs 70.8%).

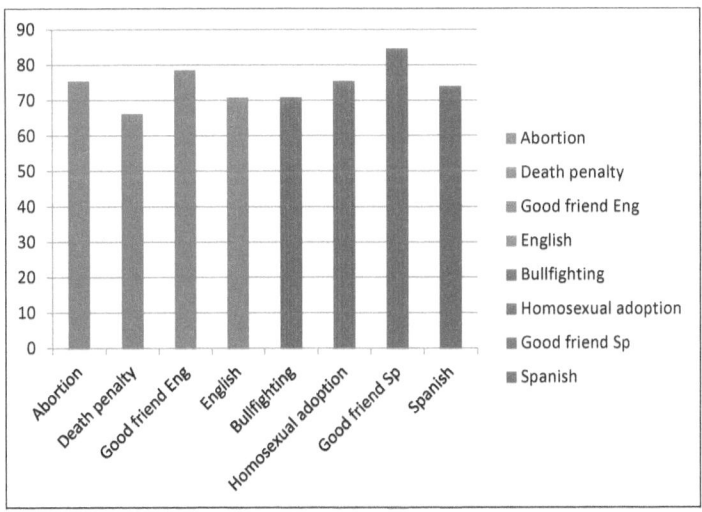

Figure 4.4 Classification results for all corpora

Thus, the key findings of this study are summarized as follows:

1. Overall, statistical classification methodologies with individual categories perform better than ML techniques with whole dimensions presented in Almela et al. (2013). Furthermore, the distribution of the classification results parallels that from the experiment with the whole categories.

2. The identification of predictors has proved more successful at pinpointing categories indicative of truthful statements, the most widely shared

among subcorpora being text length and $1^{st}$ person singular. On the other hand,

the strongest predictors for untruthfulness are $2^{nd}$ and $3^{rd}$ person.

# CHAPTER 5. Study 2: Low-stakes vs. high-stakes deception

## 5.1 Introduction

The present chapter deals with the analysis of Study 2, an intralingual experiment in English. These results are presented, analyzed and evaluated in order to answer the following research question:

> (1) Can ALIAS WISER find a difference between the automated linguistic detection of high-stakes data with actual statements from real criminal investigations and low-stakes, laboratory-produced deception?

It is worth noting that Study 2 has been conducted only in English because it is the only current language of ALIAS WISER[11]; thus, the two corpora analyzed are the high-stakes dataset and the low-stakes dataset in English, as described in Chapter 3. However, it is worth noting that the present author is currently involved in a project run at ALIAS Technology, LLC, led by Carole E. Chaski, PhD for the refining of the software, given its successful classification performance, as well as its adaptation to Spanish from English.

---

[11] https://aliastechnology.com/ali/

Specifically, the main aim of this research is to explore the linguistic cues to deception in low-stakes and high-stakes written language in English, performing a contrastive analysis between the English datasets described in Chapter 3, similar to the pilot study presented in Almela (2021b).

## 5.2 Data analysis

As explained in Chapter 2, ALIAS WISER is forensic computational linguistic software designed to help investigators prepare for interrogations by analyzing witness statements after the interview. The linguistic and statistical analyses conducted by this software on the data are explained in this section.

### 5.2.1 Linguistic analysis

Both datasets were analyzed using ALIAS WISER. It is worth noting that even though this tool is based on ALIAS TATTLER, not all the linguistic levels comprised by the latter are used for the former. Specifically, ALIAS TATTLER provides linguistic analysis for levels of language from characters to discourse –namely character, phonology, lexicon, semantics, syntax, and discourse levels. Basing on previous research (Chaski et al. 2014; 2015), ALIAS WISER includes algorithms exclusively at those three levels –this contrasts with LIWC, whose only focus is on themes. A comprehensive explanation of the variables cannot be provided here, as the developer has not published it yet, but it is to appear soon in Chaski (in press). However, in Table 5.1 the reader is provided

with a sample of WISER variables at each level:

| Character level | Lexical level | Semantic level |
|---|---|---|
| Raw frequency of single characters | TD*IDF frequencies of words in text in relation to a collection of texts | Entities |
| Raw frequency of character groups | Raw frequency of words in text | Themes |
| Relative frequency of single characters | Raw frequency of n-grams | Sentiment (positive, neutral, negative) in text |

Table 5.1 Sample of WISER variables

### 5.2.2 Statistical analysis

The quantification of the ground-truth data, labeled as untruthful statements or

truthful statements, was then subjected to statistical analysis. As explained in

Chapter 3, DFA was calculated with the software package IBM SPSS so as to

assess the discriminant power of the variables individually. In principle, the

DFA is claimed to impose restrictive normality assumptions on the predictors.

However, DFA is known to be robust even when these assumptions are

violated, as stated in most modern textbooks about multivariate statistics (e.g.,

Tabachnick & Fidell, 2013).

## 5.3 Results and discussion

This section addresses the results yielded by the application of the statistical classification technique implemented. As stated above, the statistical classification techniques applied help gain a deeper understanding of the specific categories which best discriminate between both sublanguages. First, the results are presented for the high-stakes dataset and then for the low-stakes dataset.

### *5.3.1 Results: High-stakes dataset*

DFA with leave-one-out cross-validation was first conducted on the linguistic variables extracted from Sgt. Barksdale's dataset (see Chapter 3 for a full description). As shown in Table 5.2, the analysis yielded very good results for the classification of the high-stakes dataset, similar to VeriPol (Quijano-Sánchez et al., 2018), at 91.4% cross-validated accuracy. Specifically, the algorithm correctly classified the 28 truthful texts, and 5 out of the 7 untruthful texts.

| DFA Accuracy | Truthful Docs | Hits Truthful | Misses Truthful | Untruthful Docs | Hits Untruthful | Misses Untruthful |
|---|---|---|---|---|---|---|
| 91.4% | 28 | 28 | 0 | 7 | 5 | 2 |

Table 5.2. Results from high-stakes dataset

The DFA has selected only 4 variables that work really well on the high-stakes data (Table 5.3). They are related to the linguistic expression of purpose, the ratio of 1st person singular pronouns to 3rd person pronouns, futurity and desire.

| Test | Variables in the analysis |
|------|---------------------------|
| Leave-one-out Cross Validation | Purpose |
| | Ratio of 1st person sg. pronouns to 3rd person pronouns |
| | Function words – Future |
| | Content words – Desire |

Table 5.3 Variables in the analysis of high-stakes dataset

### 5.3.2 Results: Low-stakes dataset

As could be expected, on the low-stakes dataset from Mihalcea & Strapparava (2009) fully described in Chapter 3, the accuracy of the classifier is not as high as with the high-stakes dataset. The results can be seen in Table 5.4. As this corpus is balanced and larger than the high-stakes dataset, it was possible to analyze the three subcorpora independently so as to explore differences between topics.

113

| Data | DFA Accuracy | Truthful Docs | Hits Truthful | Misses Truthful | Untruthful Docs | Hits Untruthful | Misses Untruthful |
|---|---|---|---|---|---|---|---|
| MS Data - Abortion | 71.00% | 100 | 70 | 30 | 100 | 72 | 28 |
| MS Data - Death Penalty | 69.50% | 100 | 67 | 33 | 100 | 72 | 28 |
| MS Data - Good Friend | 82.50% | 100 | 82 | 18 | 100 | 83 | 17 |

Table 5.4 Results from low-stakes dataset

On a par with the results reported in Chapter 4 both for English and Spanish, the best results on low-stakes deception may be attributed to the fact that when speakers refer to a good friend, they are more likely to be emotionally involved in the experiment. The participants are not just giving an opinion on a topic which may be alien to them, but relating their personal experience with a dear friend and lying about a person they really dislike. In line with previous research (e.g., Almela, 2021; Newman et al., 2003), their personal involvement is reflected on the linguistic expression of deception. Specifically, the algorithm correctly classified virtually the same amount of truthful and untruthful texts on good friends: 82 out of 100 truthful texts, and 83 out of 100 untruthful texts, which yields an accuracy rate of 82.5% (Table 5.4). Nonetheless, the classification was less successful with the other two topics; namely, in the abortion subcorpus only 70 out of 100 truthful texts and 72 untruthful texts out of 100 were correctly classified (71% accuracy rate), and the results were slightly poorer for death penalty: only 67 truthful texts out of 100 and 72 out of 100 untruthful texts (69.5% accuracy rate).

The DFA selected 7 variables for the classification model on the abortion corpus, shown in Table 5.5.

| Data | Variables in the analysis |
|---|---|
| MS Data - Abortion | Content words – Cognition |
| | Punctuation – Triple period |
| | Phonology – Stops |
| | Content words – Negative relations |
| | Content words – Automobile |
| | Function words – $1^{st}$ person sg. pronouns |
| | Content words – Clothing |

Table 5.5 Variables in the analysis of the abortion dataset

A different set of 7 variables was selected for the classification model on the death penalty corpus, shown in Table 5.6. The predictor $1^{st}$ person singular pronouns was included in both models, abortion and death penalty corpora.

| Data | Variables in the analysis |
|---|---|
| MS Data - Death Penalty | Function words – $1^{st}$ person sg. pronouns |
| | Phonology – Glides |
| | Function words – Purpose |
| | Punctuation – Comma |
| | Content words – Food |
| | Ratio of $1^{st}$ person pl. pronouns to other pronouns |
| | Content words – Truth |

Table 5.6 Variables in the analysis of the death penalty dataset

.

Last, Table 5.7 shows the set of 14 variables which proved meaningful in the analysis of the good friend corpus. Two of the variables had been also found in the two previous analyses, namely triple period and food.

| Data | Variables in the analysis |
|---|---|
| MS Data - Good Friend | Function words – 3$^{rd}$ person pronouns |
| | Content words – Positive relations |
| | Content words – Numbers |
| | Phonology – Labials |
| | Function words – Concessive |
| | Punctuation – Triple period |
| | Content words – Discourse Strategies for exemplifying |
| | Phonology – Back Vowels |
| | Punctuation – Single period |
| | Content words – Food |
| | Punctuation – Left parenthesis |
| | Content words – Interjections |
| | Content words – Location |
| | Function words – 2$^{nd}$ person pronouns |

Table 5.7 Variables in the analysis of the good friend dataset

### 5.3.3 Summary of results

The key findings of this study are summarized as follows:

1. Overall, DFA with ALIAS WISER categories perform strongly on high-stakes data, whereas low-stakes deception has proven harder to detect. Regarding the latter corpus, the distribution of the classification results parallels

that from the experiment reported in Chapter 4, the good friend subcorpus being the most successful one (see Figure 5.1).

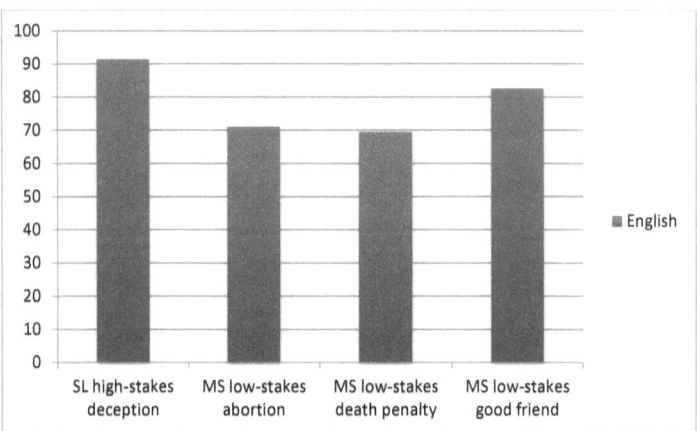

Figure 5.1 Classification results for corpora in English

2. The only WISER predictor common to high and low stakes deception is the linguistic expression of purpose. For the former dataset, three further predictors were included in the classification model, namely the ratio of 1st person singular pronouns to 3rd person pronouns, futurity and desire. As far as the low-stakes dataset is concerned, the most consistent predictors across topics were 1st person sg. pronouns, food, and triple period.

# CHAPTER 6. Final remarks, limitations of the study and further research

## 6.1 Final remarks

The results of the cross-linguistic study and the intralinguistic study suggest that low-stakes lies are more difficult to detect than high-stakes lies. In fact, low-stakes deception may be difficult to detect because it is part of the social lubricant that speakers use everyday, and so these lies seem to blend into truthful conversation, while high-stakes deception is comparatively rare. Even in the high-stakes dataset used in Chapter 5, there were far more truthful witness statements than untruthful ones.

As far as low-stakes deception is concerned, the key findings from Study 1 reveal that the statistical classification experiments with LIWC variables and the stylometric dimension perform efficiently, with a maximum success rate of 78.5% for English and 84.6% for Spanish. The results also confirm that there is a set of linguistic cues which contributes to the statistical classification models in English and in Spanish. Of interest, the identification of predictors has proved more successful at identifying linguistic cues to truthfulness instead of deception. Specifically, the shared categories are text length, self-references, insight, exclusive words, and friends. On the other hand, the other-references predictor has proved the most powerful one for deception. There are also certain cues specific to each language, and, most significantly, several discursive differences among topics, which confirms the importance of the study of deception within the specific context in which it is produced. In addition to this, the new set of stylometric features first tested in the present study has not proved significant for the individual analysis, although it has outperformed the SVM algorithms applied on the same data in Almela et al. (2013), especially in English. Other promising variables, like lexical richness and average word length, have not proved significant for the discrimination between truthful and untruthful texts. As stated by Mann et al., these findings "challenge the simplistic view, even expressed by professional lie catchers (Ekman, 1992; Vrij et al., 2000), that a typical of deceptive behavior exists" (2002: 372). This statement is closely related to the importance of establishing a baseline in behavior against which any subsequent finding may be contrasted. These individual differences have often been neglected in previous research on deception detection, hence the need for further insight, as highlighted in studies such as Vivancos-Vicente et al. (2020).

As regards ALIAS WISER, Study 2 confirms that it currently attains over 90% accuracy distinguishing truthful from false witness statements from actual criminal investigations. However, the Institute for Linguistic Evidence will keep on conducting research on new text collections to determine under what conditions this method can continue this high level of accuracy. As stated above, although some relatively successful experiments have been reported according to the emotional involvement of the authors on low-stakes data, research on high-stakes, real-life type of data have proved more successful than results on low-stakes, laboratory-produced data.

All in all, it is hoped that the present research monograph deepens human understanding of the linguistic mechanisms underlying deceit.

## 6.2 Limitations of the study

It may be argued that the main limitation of the present study is the nature of the deceptive language compiled for the Spanish corpus, since it is not spontaneously produced language, which does not seem the ideal condition for the projection of the results on a real-life sample of language. Participants were perfectly aware of the fact that their interlocutor knew that they were telling lies, and for this reason they were supposedly not interested in convincing anyone of a fake truth. In addition, the original motivation behind their lying was not a real world one, like rejecting a charge. However, participants had to make sure that they were able to convince their recipient on the topics that they were lying about, and the Hawthorne effect was minimized by not explicitly telling the participants the ultimate aim of the study.

Moreover, as has been seen, criminal proceedings do not always offer a verbatim transcript of the liar's words; thus, the only available option for the study of high-stakes written deception seems to be forensic written statements. In civil law jurisdictions, this is not the usual procedure, hence the major difficulty of finding the kind of material used for the English corpus in Study 2. Even so, it must be acknowledged that the high-stakes corpus used in the latter study is of limited size in comparison to the ones comprising low-stakes deception.

Furthermore, a proper control of any intervening variables in the experiment would have entailed two datasets with exactly the same topics in both languages. In Study 1, just one of the subject matters is shared, namely good friend, whereas the other two topics in Spanish, bullfighting and homosexual adoption, differ from the original English corpus. The two new subjects were selected because they were highly topical and controversial in the source country, namely Spain, and they were considered to actively involve participants in their discussion. Nonetheless, it must be acknowledged that two suitably comparable corpora would have enabled a direct cross-linguistic comparison, as it is the case with the English and Spanish good friend subcorpora.

## 6.3 Further research

Regarding Study 1, it may be the starting point for further comparisons between other pairs of languages, in order to identify possible structural and lexical differences between the linguistic expression of deceit across two languages.

As far as ALIAS WISER is concerned, the Institute for Linguistic Evidence is conducting ongoing research on new text collections to determine under what conditions WISER can continue the high level of accuracy reported on the high-stakes dataset analyzed in Study 2. Furthermore, there is an ongoing research agenda for the WISER project, which includes getting

121

Spanish translations of ALIAS categories, and getting enough witness statements for high-stakes ground-truth data in Spanish, implementing a protocol similar to that reported in Quijano-Sánchez et al. (2018).

Finally, a further line of research could delve into the cognitive linguistic aspects of deception, as suggested by certain findings commented on in the present study. Since metaphorical language is often used to disclaim responsibility for the conveyed message, it would certainly be interesting to explore the extent to which it is used in deceptive communication.

# REFERENCES

Adams, S. H., & Jarvis, J. P. (2006). Indicators of veracity and deception: an analysis of written statements made to police. *International Journal of speech language and the law,* *13*(1), 1–22. doi.org/10.1558/SLL.2006.13.1.1

Ali, M., & Levine, T. (2008). The language of truthful and deceptive denials and confessions. *Communication Reports,* *21*(2), 82–91. doi.org/10.1080/08934210802381862

Almela, A. (2021a). A corpus-based study of linguistic deception in Spanish. *Applied Sciences,* *11*(19), 1–22. doi.org/10.3390/app11198817

Almela, A. (2021b). Computational Classification of Written Statements as True or False: Comparing Experimental and High-Stakes Data in the Forensic Setting. Oral presentation given at the *2021 AAFS Annual Scientific Meeting,* Houston, TX.

Almela, A., Alcaraz-Mármol, G., & Cantos, P. (2015). Analysing deception in a psychopath's speech: A quantitative approach. *DELTA: Documentação de Estudos em Lingüística Teórica e Aplicada,* *31*(2), 559–572. doi.org/10.1590/0102-445040702531513856

Almela, A., Alcaraz-Mármol, G., García-Pinar, A., & Pallejá, C. (2019). Developing and analyzing a Spanish corpus for forensic purposes. *LESLI: Linguistic Evidence in Security, Law and Intelligence,* *3,* 1–13. doi.org/10.5195/lesli.2019.19

Almela, A., Berber-Sardinha, T., & Cantos, P. (2022). Métodos multidimensionales basados en corpus del español [Multidimensional methods based on Spanish corpora]. In G. Parodi, P. Cantos, and C. Howe, *Lingüística de corpus en español* [*The Routledge Handbook of Spanish Corpus Linguistics*] (pp. 545–557). London: Routledge.

Almela, A., Valencia-García, R., & Cantos, P. (2012). Detectando la mentira en lenguaje escrito [Detecting deception in written language]. *Procesamiento de Lenguaje Natural, 48,* 65–72.

Almela, A., Valencia-García, R., & Cantos, P. (2013). Seeing through deception: A computational approach to deceit detection in written communication. *LESLI: Linguistic Evidence in Security, Law and Intelligence, 1*(1), 3–12. doi.org/10.5195/lesli.2013.5

Anolli, L., Balconi, M., & Ciceri, R. (2002). Deceptive Miscommunication Theory (DeMiT): A new model for the analysis of deceptive communication. In L. Anolli, R. Ciceri & G. Riva (Eds.), *Say Not to Say: New Perspectives in Miscommunication* (pp. 73–100). IOS Press.

Anolli, L., & Ciceri, R. (1997). The voice of deception: Vocal strategies of naive and able liars. *Journal of Nonverbal Behavior, 21*(4), 259–284. doi.org/10.1023/A:1024916214403

Aparicio, L. (2010). La mentira, ¿un derecho del imputado? [Lies, a defendant's right?]. *La Toga Digital, 180,* 48–50.

Arce, R., & Fariña, F. (2006). Psicología del testimonio y evaluación cognitiva de la veracidad de testimonios y declaraciones [The psychology of testimony and the cognitive assessment of the veracity of testimonies and statements]. In J. C. Sierra, E. M. Jiménez, and G. Buela-Casal (Eds.), *Psicología Forense: Manual de Técnicas y Aplicaciones* (pp. 563 601). Madrid: Biblioteca Nueva.

Babbie, E. R. (2009). *The Practice of Social Research* (12th ed.). Belmont, California: Wadsworth Publishing.

Bagaric, M. (1997). The diminishing "right" of silence. *Sydney Law Review*, 19, 366.

Bedwell, J. S., Gallagher, S., Whitten, S. N., & Fiore, S. M. (2011). Linguistic correlates of self in deceptive oral autobiographical narratives. *Consciousness and Cognition, 20*(3), 547–555. doi.org/10.1016/j.concog.2010.10.001

Berber-Sardinha, T., & Veirano-Pinto, M. (Eds.). (2019). *Multi-dimensional analysis: Research methods and current issues*. London: Bloomsbury Publishing.

Böhm, C., & Steller, M. (2008). Testimonio y trastorno límite de personalidad [Testimony and borderline personality disorder]. In F. J. Rodríguez, C. Bringas, F. Fariña, R. Arce, and A. Bernardo (Eds.), *Psicología Jurídica. Entorno judicial y delincuencia* (pp. 135–147). Ediciones de la Universidad de Oviedo.

Bond Jr., C. F., & Robinson, M. (1988). The evolution of deception. *Journal of Nonverbal Behavior, 12*(4), 295–307. doi.org/10.1007/BF00987597

Bradley, M. T., & Janisse, M. P. (1981). Accuracy demonstrations, threat, and the detection of deception: Cardiovascular, electrodermal, and papillary measures. *Psychophysiology, 18*(3), 307–315. doi.org/10.1111/j.1469-8986.1981.tb03040.x

Brown, J. D., & Rodgers, T. S. (2002). *Doing second language research: An introduction to the theory and practice of second language research for graduate/master's students in TESOL and applied linguistics, and others.* Oxford: Oxford University Press.

Brownsell, A., & Bull, R. (2011). Magistrates' beliefs concerning verbal and non-verbal behaviours as indicators of deception. *European Journal of Psychology Applied to Legal Context, 3*(1), 29–46.

Bull, R. (1997). Entrevistas a niños testigos [Interviews to child witnesses]. In F. Fariña & R. Arce (Eds.), *Psicología e investigación judicial* (pp. 19–38). Madrid: Fundación Universidad Empresa.

Bull, R., Cook, C., Hatcher, R., Woodhams, J., Bilby, C., & Grant, T. (2006). *Criminal Psychology: A Beginner's Guide.* Oxford: Oneworld Publications.

Buller, D. B., & Burgoon, J. K. (1996). Interpersonal deception theory. *Communication Theory, 6*(3), 203–242. doi.org/10.1111/j.1468-2885.1996.tb00127.x

Burdick, F. M. (1905/2000). *The Law of Torts: A Concise Treatise on the Civil Liability at Common Law and Under Modern Statutes for Actionable Wrongs to Person and Property.* Beard Books.

Burgoon, J. K., Buller, D. B., & Woodall, W. G. (1996). *Nonverbal communication: The unspoken dialogue.* McGraw-Hill College.

Campbell, R. S., & Pennebaker, J. W. (2003). The secret life of pronouns: Flexibility in writing style and physical health. *Psychological Science, 14*(1), 60–65. doi.org/10.1111/1467-9280.01419

Cantos, P. (2013). *Statistical Methods in Language and Linguistic Research.* Sheffield: Equinox.

Cantos, P., & Almela, A. (2019). Readability indices for the assessment of textbooks: A feasibility study in the context of EFL. *Vigo International Journal of Applied Linguistics, 16*, 31–52. doi.org/10.35869/vial.v0i16

Carney, M. W., Chary, T. K., Robotis, P., & Childs, A. (1987). Ganser syndrome and its management. *The British Journal of Psychiatry: the journal of mental science, 151*(5), 697–700. doi.org/10.1192/bjp.151.5.697

Castelfranchi, C., & Poggi, I. (2002). *Bugie, finzioni, sotterfugi [Lies, fictions, subterfuges].* Roma : Carocci.

Chaski, C. E. (2001). Empirical evaluations of language-based author identification techniques. *Forensic Linguistics, 8*(1), 1–65.

Chaski, C. E. (2012). Author identification in the forensic setting. In L. M. Solan & P. M. Tiersma (Eds.), *The Oxford Handbook of Language and Law* (pp. 489-503). Oxford University Press. doi.org/10.1093/oxfordhb/9780199572120.013.0036

Chaski, C. E. (2013). Best practices and admissibility of forensic author identification. *Journal of Law and Policy, 21*(2), 332–376.

Chaski, C. E. (2021). Deception Data, Mindset, and Validation Testing. Oral presentation given at the *2021 AAFS Annual Scientific Meeting*, Houston, TX.

Chaski, C. E. (in press). A Primer of Forensic Computational Linguistics for Analysis of Significant Texts in Psychiatry. *Journal of Scientific Exploration, 37*(2).

Chaski, C. E., Almela, A., Holness, G., & Barksdale, L. (2015). WISER: Automatically Classifying Written Statements as True or False. In *Proceedings of the American Academy of Forensic Sciences 67th Annual Scientific Meeting*, Orlando, FL, USA (pp. 576–577).

Chaski, C. E., Barksdale, L., & Reddington, M. M. (2014). Collecting Forensic Linguistic Data: Police and Investigative Sources of Data for Deception Detection Research. In *Proceedings of the Linguistic Society of America Annual Meeting*, Minneapolis, MN, USA (pp. 2–5).

Chipere, N., Malvern, D., & Richards, B. J. (2004). Using a corpus of children's writing to test a solution to the sample size problem affecting type-token ratios. In G. Aston, S. Bernardini & D. Stewart (Eds.), *Corpora and language learners* (pp. 139–147). Amsterdam: John Benjamins.

Cohen, J. (1988). Set Correlation and Contingency Tables. *Applied Psychological Measurement,* *12*(4), 425–434. doi:10.1177/014662168801200410

Cohen, J., Cohen, P., West, S. G., & Aiken, L. S. (2002). *Applied multiple regression/correlation analysis for the behavioral sciences* (3rd ed.). London: Routledge. doi.org/10.4324/9780203774441

Coulthard, M. (1994). On the use of corpora in the analysis of forensic texts. *International Journal of Speech, Language and Law, 1*(1), 27–43.

Dalla Barba, G. (1993). Confabulation: Knowledge and recollective experience. *Cognitive Neuropsychology,* *10*(1), 1–20. doi.org/10.1080/02643299308253454

Deese, J. (1965). *The Structure of Associations in Language and Thought.* Baltimore: The John Hopkins Press.

Deese, J. (1969). Conceptual Categories in the Study of Content. In G. Gerbner, O. R. Holsti, K. Krippendorf, W. J. Paisley and P. J. Stone (Eds), *The Analysis of Communication Content* (pp. 39–56). New York: John Wiley & Sons, Inc.

DePaulo, B. M., Kashy, D. A., Kirkendol, S. E., Wyer, M. M., & Epstein, J. A. (1996). Lying in everyday life. *Journal of Personality and Social Psychology, 70*(5), 979–995. doi.org/10.1037/0022-3514.70.5.979

DePaulo, B. M., & Kirkendol, S. E. (1989). The motivational impairment effect in the communication of deception. In J. C. Yuille (Ed.), *Credibility assessment* (pp. 51–70). Dordrecht, the Netherlands: Kluwer.

DePaulo, B. M., Lindsay, J. J., Malone, B. E., Muhlenbruck, L., Charlton, K., & Cooper, H. (2003). Cues to deception. *Psychological Bulletin, 129*(1), 74–118. doi.org/10.1037/0033-2909.129.1.74

Derrick, D., Meservy, T., Burgoon, J., & Nunamaker, J. (2012). An experimental agent for detecting deceit in chat-based communication. In *Proceedings of the Rapid Screening Technologies, Deception Detection and Credibility Assessment Symposium* (pp. 5–13). Grand Wailea Maui, HI.

*DSM IV–TR: Diagnostic and Statistical Manual of Mental Disorders* (2000), 4th ed. American Psychiatric Association.

Dike, C. C. (2008). Pathological Lying: Symptom or disease? Living with no permanent motive or benefit. *Psychiatric Times, 25*(7), 67. http://www.psychiatrictimes.com/display/article/10168/1162950

Efron, B., Hastie, T., Johnstone, I., & Tibshirani, R. (2004). Least angle regression. *The Annals of Statistics, 32*(2), 407–451. doi.org/10.1214/009053604000000067

Ekman, P. (1985). *Telling lies.* New York: W. W. Norton and Company.

Ekman, P. (1992). *Telling lies: Clues to deceit in the marketplace, politics, and marriage* (2nd ed.). New York: W. W. Norton and Company.

Ekman, P., & Friesen, W. V. (1969). Nonverbal leakage and clues to deception. *Psychiatry, 32*(1), 88–105. doi.org/10.1080/00332747.1969.11023575

Etienne, M. (2005). The ethics of cause lawyering: An empirical examination of criminal defense lawyers as cause lawyers. *The Journal of Criminal Law and Criminology, 95*(4), 1195–1260.

Faigman, D. L., Fienberg, S. E., & Stern, P. C. (2003). Limits of the polygraph. *Issues in Science and Technology, 20*(1), 40-46.

Farwell, L. A., & Donchin, E. (1991). The truth will out: Interrogative polygraphy ("lie detection") with event-related brain potentials. *Psychophysiology,* *28*(5), 531–47. doi.org/10.1111/j.1469-8986.1991.tb01990.x

Feldman, M. D., Ford, C. V., & Reinhold, T. (1993). *Patient or pretender: Inside the strange world of factitious disorders.* John Wiley and Sons Inc.

Feng, S., Banerjee, R., & Choi, Y. (2012). Syntactic stylometry for deception detection. In *Proceedings of the 50th Annual Meeting of the Association for Computational Linguistics* (pp. 171–175). Korea: Association for Computational Linguistics.

Fitzpatrick, E., & Bachenko, J. (2010). Building a forensic corpus to test language-based indicators of deception. In S. T. Gries, S. Wulff & M. Davies (Eds.), *Language and computers, special issue corpus–linguistic applications: Current Studies, new directions* (pp. 183–196). doi.org/10.1163/9789042028012_013

Fitzpatrick, E., & Bachenko, J. (2013). Detecting Deception across Linguistically Diverse Text Types. In *Proceedings of the Linguistic Society of America Annual Meeting*, Boston, MA, USA.

Fitzpatrick, E., Bachenko, J., & Fornaciari, T. (2015). *Automatic Detection of Verbal Deception. Synthesis Lectures or Human Language Technologies.* Williston (VT): Morgan and Claypool Publishers.

Ford, C. V. (1999). *Lies! Lies! Lies! The psychology of deceit, relation of neurological dysfunction to deceit.* American Psychiatric Press.

Fornaciari, T., & Poesio, M. (2011). Lexical vs. Surface Features in Deceptive Language Analysis. In A. Wyner and K. Branting (Eds.), *Proceedings of the ICAIL 2011 Workshop Applying Human Language Technology to the Law.* University of Pittsburgh School of Law. http://wyner.info/research/Papers/AHLTL2011Papers.pdf

Fornaciari, T., & Poesio, M. (2013). Automatic deception detection in Italian court cases. *Artificial Intelligence and Law, 21*(3), 303–340.

Fuller, C. M., Biros, D. P., Burgoon, J. K., Adkins, M., & Twitchell, D. P. (2006). An analysis of text-based deception detection tools. In *Proceedings of the Twelfth Americas Conference on Information Systems* (p. 418).

Gamer, M., Rill, H. G., Vossel, G., & Gödert, H. W. (2006). Psychophysiological and vocal measures in the detection of guilty knowledge. *International Journal of Psychophysiology, 60*(1), 76–87. doi.org/10.1016/j.ijpsycho.2005.05.006

Gibbs, R. (1994). *The Poetics of Mind: Figurative Thought, Language and Understanding.* New York: Cambridge University Press.

Goldhamer, D. H. (1969). Toward a More General Inquirer: Convergence of Structure. In G. Gerbner, O. R. Holsti, K. Krippendorf, W. J. Paisley and P. J. Stone (Eds), *The Analysis of Communication Content* (pp. 343 353). New York: John Wiley & Sons, Inc.

Graesser, A. C., McNamara, D. S., Louwerse, M. M., & Cai, Z. (2004). Coh-Metrix: Analysis of text on cohesion and language. *Behavior research methods, instruments, & computers, 36*(2), 193–202. doi.org/10.3758/BF03195564

Granhag, P. A., Strömwall, L. A., & Olsson, C. (2001). Fact or fiction? Adults' ability to assess children's veracity. Paper presented at the *11th European Conference on Psychology and Law*, Lisbon, Portugal.

Guilford, J. P. (1954). *Psychometric Methods.* New York: McGraw-Hill.

Hancock, J. T., Thom–Santelli, J., & Ritchie, T. (2004). Deception and design: The impact of communication technologies on lying behavior. In *Proceedings of the ACM Conference on Human Factors in Computing Systems (CHI 2004),* 6 (pp. 130–136). New York: ACM.

Hancock, J. T., Woodworth, M., & Goorha, S. (2010). See no evil: The effect of communication medium and motivation on deception detection. *Group Decision and Negotiation, 19*(4), 327–343. doi.org/10.1007/s10726-009-9169-7

Hare, R. D., Forth, A. E., & Hart, S. D. (1989). The psychopath as prototype for pathological lying and deception. In J. C. Yuille (Ed.), *Credibility*

*assessment*     (pp.     25–49).     Dordrecht:     Kluwer.
https://psycnet.apa.org/doi/10.1007/978-94-015-7856-1_2

Harris, Z. S. (1954). Distributional structure. *Word, 10*(2-3), 146–162.
doi.org/10.1080/00437956.1954.11659520

Hartwig, M., Granhag, P. A., Stromwall, L. A., & Kronvist, O. (2006).
Strategic use of evidence during police interviews: When training to
detect deception works. *Law and Human Behavior, 30*(5), 603–619.
https://psycnet.apa.org/doi/10.1007/s10979-006-9053-9

Hauch, V., Blandón-Gitlin, I., Masip, J., & Sporer, S. L. (2015). Are computers
effective lie detectors? A meta-analysis of linguistic cues to deception.
*Personality and Social Psychology Review, 19*(4), 307–342.
doi.org/10.1177%2F1088868314556539

Hausman, K. (2003). Does pathological lying warrant inclusion in DSM?
*American Psychiatric Association, 38*(1), 24.
doi.org/10.1176/pn.38.1.0024

Healy, W., & Healy, M. T. (1969). *Pathological lying, accusation, and
swindling: A study in forensic psychology.* Montclair, NJ: Paterson Smith.

Honts, C. R., Hodes, R. L., & Raskin, D. C. (1985). Effects of physical
countermeasures on the physiological detection of deception. *Journal of
Applied Psychology, 70*(1), 177.

Honts, C. R., & Kircher, J. C. (1994). Mental and physical countermeasures
reduce the accuracy of polygraph tests. *Journal of Applied
Psychology, 79*(2), 252.

Hosmer, D. W., & Lemeshow, S. (2000). *Applied logistic regression* (2$^{nd}$ ed.). John Wiley & Sons.

Jensen, M. L. (2007). *The effects of an expert system on novice and professional decision making with application in deception detection* [Unpublished PhD dissertation]. University of Arizona. https://www.proquest.com/dissertations-theses/effects-expert-system-on-novice-professional/docview/304894882/se-2?accountid=14620

Juola, P. (2015). The Rowling Case: A Proposed Standard Analytic Protocol for Authorship Questions. *Digital Scholarship in the Humanities, 30*(1), 100–113. doi.org/10.1093/llc/fqv040

Jurafsky, D., & Martin, J. H. (2021). *Speech and language Processing: An introduction to natural language processing, computational linguistics, and speech recognition* (3$^{rd}$ Ed.). Stanford University. https://web.stanford.edu/~jurafsky/slp3/

Kagan, S. (1998). *Normative Ethics*. Boulder: Westview Press.

Kang, S. M., & Lee, H. (2014). Detecting deception by analyzing written statements in Korean. *Linguistic Evidence in Security, Law and Intelligence, 2*(2), 1–10. doi.org/10.5195/lesli.2014.13

Kassin, S. M., Meissner, C. A., & Norwick, R. J. (2005). "I'd Know a False Confession if I Saw One": A Comparative Study of College Students and Police Investigators. *Law and Human Behavior, 29*(2), 211–227. doi.org/10.1007/s10979-005-2416-9

Kline, P. (1986). *A handbook of test construction.* New York: Methuen.

Knapp, M. L., Hart, R. P., & Dennis, H. S. (1974). An exploration of deception as a communication construct. *Human Communication Research, 1*(1), 15–29. doi.org/10.1111/j.1468-2958.1974.tb00250.x

Kövecses, Z. (2000). *Metaphor and emotion: Language, culture, and body in human feeling.* Cambridge: Cambridge University Press.

Kraut, R. E. (1978). Verbal and nonverbal cues in the perception of lying. *Journal of Personality and Social Psychology, 36*(4), 380–391. https://psycnet.apa.org/doi/10.1037/0022-3514.36.4.380

Lesce, T. (1990). Scan: Deception detection by scientific content analysis. *Law and Order, 38*(8), 3–6. http://www.lsiscan.com/id37.htm

Levy, L. W. (1969). *Origins of the Fifth Amendment.* New York: Macmillan.

Mahon, J. E. (2015). The definition of lying and deception. In E. N. Zalta (Ed.), *The Stanford Encyclopedia of Philosophy.* http://plato.stanford.edu/archives/fall2008/entries/lying–definition/

Mann, S., Vrij, A., & Bull, R. (2002). Suspects, lies, and videotape: An analysis of authentic high-stake liars. *Law and Human Behavior, 26*(3), 365–376. doi.org/10.1023/A:1015332606792

Markowitz, D. M., & Hancock, J. T. (2019). Deception and Language: The Contextual organization of Language and Deception (CoLD) framework. In T. Docan-Morgan (Ed.), *The Palgrave Handbook of Deceptive Communication* (pp. 193–212). New York: Palgrave Macmillan.

McCarney, R., Warner, J., Iliffe, S., van Haselen, R., Griffin, M., & Fisher, P. (2007). The Hawthorne Effect: A randomised, controlled trial. *BMC Medical Research Methodology*, *7*(1), 1–8. doi.org/10.1186/1471-2288-7-30

McNamara, D. S., Graesser, A. C., McCarthy, P. M., & Cai, Z. (2014). *Automated evaluation of text and discourse with Coh-Metrix*. Cambridge: Cambridge University Press.

Meibauer, J. (Ed.). (2018). *The Oxford Handbook of Lying*. Oxford: Oxford University Press.

Memon, A., Fraser, J., Colwel, K., Odinot, G., & Mastroberardino, S. (2010). Distinguishing truthful from invented accounts using Reality Monitoring criteria. *Legal and Criminological Psychology*, *15*(2), 177–194. doi.org/10.1348/135532508X401382

Menard, S. (1995). *Applied logistic regression analysis*. Thousand Oaks: Sage.

Meservy, T. (2007). *Augmenting human intellect: Automatic recognition of nonverbal behavior with application in deception detection* [Unpublished doctoral dissertation]. University of Arizona. https://www.proquest.com/dissertations-theses/augmenting-human-intellect-automatic-recognition/docview/304895587/se-2?accountid=14620

Mihalcea, R., & Strapparava, C. (2009). The Lie Detector: Explorations in the Automatic Recognition of Deceptive Language. In *Proceedings of the*

*Association for Computational Linguistics, ACL-IJCNLP 2009* (pp. 309–312), Singapore.

Miller, G. R., & Stiff, J. B. (1993). *Deceptive communication*. Newbury Park, CA: Sage Publications.

Mitkov, R. (2003). *Oxford Handbook of Computational Linguistics*. Oxford: Oxford University Press.

Newman, M., Pennebaker, J., Berry, D., & Richards, J. (2003). Lying words: Predicting deception from linguistic styles. *Personality and Social Psychology Bulletin, 29*(5), 665–675. doi.org/10.1177%2F0146167203029005010

Ott, M., Choi, Y., Cardie, C., & Hancock, J.T. (2011). Finding deceptive opinion spam by any stretch of the imagination. In *Proceedings of the 49th Annual Meeting of the Association for Computational Linguistics: Human Language Technologies* (pp. 309–319). Portland, OR: Association for Computational Linguistics.

Pavlidis, I., & Levine, J. (2002). Thermal image analysis for polygraph testing. *IEEE Engineering in Medicine and Biology Magazine, 21*(6), 56–64. doi.org/10.1109/MEMB.2002.1175139

Pennebaker, J. W., & King, L. A. (1999). Linguistic styles: Language use as an individual difference. *Journal of Personality and Social Psychology, 77*(6), 1296–1312. doi/10.1037/0022-3514.77.6.1296

Pennebaker, J. W., & Graybeal, A. (2001). Patterns of natural language use: Disclosure, personality, and social integration. *Current Directions in*

*Psychological Science, 10*(3), 90–93. doi.org/10.1111%2F1467-8721.00123

Pennebaker, J. W., Francis, M. E., & Booth, R. J. (2001). *Linguistic inquiry and word count.* Erlbaum Publishers.

Pérez-Rosas, V., & Mihalcea, R. (2015). Experiments in open domain deception detection. In *Proceedings of the 2015 Conference on Empirical Methods in Natural Language Processing* (pp. 1120–1125). Lisbon: Association for Computational Linguistics.

Picornell, I. (2012). *Cues to deception in a textual narrative context: Lying in written witness statements* [PhD dissertation]. Birmingham: Aston University.

Picornell, I. (2013). Analysing deception in written witness statements. *Linguistic Evidence in Security, Law and Intelligence, 1*(1), 41–50. doi.org/10.5195/lesli.2013.2

Quijano-Sánchez, L., Liberatore, F., Camacho-Collados, J., & Camacho-Collados, M. (2018). Applying automatic text-based detection of deceptive language to police reports: Extracting behavioral patterns from a multi-step classification model to understand how we lie to the police. *Knowledge-Based Systems, 149,* 155–168. doi.org/10.1016/j.knosys.2018.03.010

Ramírez-Esparza, N., Pennebaker, J. W., & García, F.A. (2007). La psicología del uso de las palabras: Un programa de computadora que analiza textos en español [The psychology of word use: A computer program that analyzes texts in Spanish]. *Revista Mexicana de Psicología, 24*(1), 85–99.

Ríos, G. A. (2019). ¿Tiene el imputado el derecho a mentir? El derecho a la verdad y el deber de declararla [Has the defendant the right to lie? The right to the truth and the duty to declare it]. *CES Derecho, 10*(2), 641–653.

Rubin, V.L., & Vashchilko, T. (2012). Identification of truth and deception in text: Application of vector space model to rhetorical structure theory. In *Proceedings of the Workshop on Computational Approaches to Deception Detection* (pp. 97–106). Avignon: Association for Computational Linguistics.

Ruby, C. L., & Brigham, J. C. (1994). *The Criteria-Based Content Analysis and its Utility in Distinguishing between Truthful and Fabricated Criminal Allegations: A Critical Review.* DTIC report. Department of the Air Force – Florida State University.

Salas-Zárate, M., López-López, E., Valencia-García, R., Aussenac-Gilles, N., Almela, Á., & Alor-Hernández, G. (2014). A study on LIWC categories for opinion mining in Spanish reviews. *Journal of Information Science, 40*(6), 749–760. doi.org/10.1177%2F0165551514547842

Salton, G., & McGill, M. (1983). *Introduction to modern information retrieval.* McGraw-Hill: New York.

Sapir, A. (1987). *Scientific Content Analysis (SCAN).* Phoenix, AZ: Laboratory of Scientific Investigation.

Scott, M. (2020a). *WordSmith Tools (Version 8)*. Stroud: Lexical Analysis Software.

Scott, M. (2020b). *WordSmith Tools Help*. Stroud: Lexical Analysis Software.

Shadish, W. R., Cook, T. D., & Campbell, D. T. (2002). *Experimental and quasi-experimental designs for generalized causal inference*. Houghton Mifflin Company

Shuy, R. (1998). *The language of confession, interrogation, and deception*. Thousand Oaks/London/Delhi: Sage.

Skillicorn, D., & Lamb, C. (2013). Extending textual models of deception to interrogation settings. *Linguistic Evidence in Security, Law and Intelligence, 1*(1), 13–40.

Snow, R., O'Connor, B., Jurafsky, D., & Ng, A. (2008). Cheap and fast – but is it good? Evaluating non-expert annotations for natural language tasks. In *Proceedings of the Conference on Empirical Methods in Natural Language Processing* (pp. 1–10).

Sporer, S. L. (1997). The less travelled road to truth: Verbal cues in deception detection in accounts of fabricated and self-experienced events. *Applied Cognitive Psychology, 11*(5), 373–397. doi.org/10.1002/(SICI)10990720(199710)11:5%3C373::AIDACP461%3E3.0.CO;20

Sporer, S. L., Manzanero, A. L., & Masip, J. (2020). Optimizing CBCA and RM research: Recommendations for analyzing and reporting data on content cues to deception. *Psychology, Crime & Law*, *27*(1), 1–39. doi.org/10.1080/1068316X.2020.1757097

Steller, M., & Köhnken, G. (1989). Criteria-based content analysis. In D. C. Raskin (Ed.), *Psychological methods in criminal investigation and evidence* (pp. 217-245). New York: Springer-Verlag.

Stone, P. J., Bales, R. F., Namenwirth, J. Z., & Ogilvie, D. M. (1962). The general inquirer: A computer system for content analysis and retrieval based on the sentence as a unit of information. *Behavioral Science*, *7*(4), 484–494.

Stone, P. J., Dunphy, D., Smith, M. S., & Ogilvie, D. M. (1966). *The general inquirer: A computer approach to content analysis.* MIT Press: Cambridge, MA, USA.

Strader, J. K. (2002). *Understanding white collar crime.* LexisNexis

Strömwall, L., & Granhag, A. (2005). Children's repeated lies and truths: Effects on adults' judgements and reality monitoring scores. *Psychiatry, Psychology and Law*, *12*(2), 345–356. doi.org/10.1375/pplt.12.2.345

Tabachnick, B. G., & Fidell, L. S. (2013). *Using multivariate statistics (New International Edition, 6th ed.).* Harlow: Pearson Education Limited.

Trankell, A. (1972). *Reliability of evidence: Methods for analyzing and assessing witness statements.* Stockholm: Beckmans.

Twitchell, D. P., Adkins, M., Nunamaker, J. F., & Burgoon, J. K. (2004). Using Speech Act Theory to Model Conversations for Automated Classification and Retrieval. Paper presented at the *Ninth International*

*Working Conference on the Language Action Perspective on Communication Modeling*, New Brunswick, NJ.

Undeutsch, U. (1967). Beurteilung der Glaubhaftigkeit von Aussagen [Veracity assessment of statements]. In U. Undeutsch (Ed.), *Handbuch der Psychologie: Forensische Psychologie* (pp. 26–181). Gottingen: Hogrefe.

Undeutsch, U. (1989). The development of statement reality analysis. In J. C. Yuille (Ed.), *Credibility Assessment* (pp. 101–119). Kluwer Academic Publishers.

Vivancos-Vicente, P. J., García-Díaz, J. A., Almela, A., Molina, F., Castejón-Garrido, J. A., & Valencia-García, R. (2020). Transcripción, indexación y análisis automático de declaraciones judiciales a partir de representaciones fonéticas y técnicas de lingüística forense. *Procesamiento del Lenguaje Natural, 65*, 109–112.

Vogler, N., & Pearl, L. (2019). Using linguistically defined specific details to detect deception across domains. *Natural Language Engineering, 26*(3), 349–373. doi.org/10.1017/S1351324919000408

Vrij, A. (2010). *Detecting lies and deceit: Pitfalls and opportunities* (2nd ed.). John Wiley and Sons.

Vrij, A., Edward, K., Roberts, K. P., & Bull, R. (2000). Detecting deceit via analysis of verbal and nonverbal behavior. *Journal of Nonverbal Behaviour, 24*(4), 239–264. doi.org/10.1023/A:1006610329284

Vrij, A., Mann, S., Fisher, R., Leal, S., Milne, R., & Bull, R. (2008). Increasing cognitive load to facilitate lie detection: The benefit of recalling an event in reverse order. *Law and Human Behavior, 32*(3), 253–265. doi.org/10.1007/s10979-007-9103-y

Yancheva, M., & Rudzicz, F. (2013). Automatic detection of deception in child-produced speech using syntactic complexity features. In *Proceedings of the 51st Annual Meeting of the Association for Computational Linguistics* (pp. 944–953). Stroudsburg, PA: Association for Computational Linguistics.

Zhou, L., Booker, Q. E., & Zhang, D. (2002). ROD: Towards rapid ontology development for underdeveloped domains. In *Proceedings of the 35th Hawaii International Conference on System Sciences* (pp. 957–965). Honolulu, HI.

Zhou, L., Burgoon, J., Nunamaker, J., & Twitchell, D. (2004). Automating linguistics-based cues for detecting deception in text–based asynchronous computer–mediated communications. *Group Decision and Negotiation, 13*(2), 81–106. doi.org/10.1023/B:GRUP.0000011944.62889.6f

Zuckerman, M., DePaulo, B. M., & Rosenthal, R. (1981). Verbal and nonverbal communication of deception. In L. Berkowitz (Ed.), *Advances in experimental social psychology* (pp. 1–59). Academic Press. doi.org/10.1016/S0065-2601(08)60369